CANADA'S
LITTLE WAR

Carman Miller

JAMES LORIMER & COMPANY LTD., PUBLISHERS

TORONTO

James Lorimer & Company Ltd. acknowledges the support of the Department of Canadian Heritage and the
Ontario Arts Council in the development of writing
and publishing in Canada.

We acknowledge the support of the Government of
Ontario through the Ontario Media Development
Corporation's Ontario Book Initiative. We acknowledge
the support of the Canada Council for the Arts for our
publishing program.

Photo credits:
Canadian War Museum (photographer: Jana
Chytilova), pp. 3, 7BL, 10TM, 11TR, 20M, 26, 28,
31, 34L, 35BR, 38BM, 40, 41M, 41BR, 46, 48, 64,
65, 69, 70, 75, 77-81, 85BM, 88, 90-95
City of Toronto Archives, Series 330, File 87, pp.
35TL, 36M
City of Toronto Archives, Series 340, subseries 4, File 7,
42TM
ML Design from Jackson, Tabitha, *The Boer War*
(London: Channel 4 Books,1999), pp 4.
National Archives of Canada, front cover, pp. 7M, 14,
25L, 29, 32, 39TL, 57, 85TM, 86

**National Library of Canada Cataloguing in
Publication**

Miller, Carman, 1940-
        Canada's little war : fighting for the British
Empire in Southern Africa,
1899-1902 / Carman Miller.

Includes bibliographical references and index.
ISBN 1-55028-800-8 (bound).—ISBN 1-55028-805-9
(pbk.)

        1. South African War, 1899-1902—
Participation, Canadian. 2. Canada.
Canadian Army—History—South African War, 1899-
1902. I. Title.

DT1913.C3M54 2003   968.04'84'0971
C2003-903622-7

James Lorimer & Company Ltd., Publishers
35 Britain Street
Toronto, Ontario
M5A 1R7
www.lorimer.ca

Distributed in the U.S. by
Casemate
2114 Darby Road, 2nd floor
Havertown, PA
19083

Printed and bound in the People's Republic of China

CONTENTS

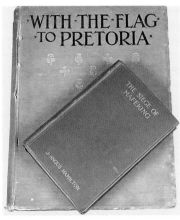

MAP OF SOUTH AFRICA

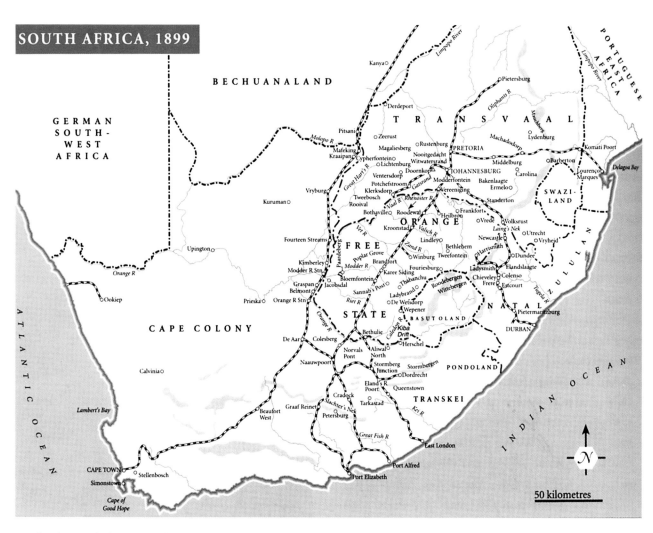

South Africa at the beginning of the Boer War

INTRODUCTION

Each year, for many years, a dwindling group of ageing men paraded to their local South African War monument. They came to remember their fallen comrades, and later to trade recollections of their service as Soldiers of the Queen in an increasingly distant conflict, soon to be overshadowed by two world wars. In 1962 they paraded for the last time. Thirty years later the last Boer War veteran died; he was 108 years old. These men left an impressive quantity of memorabilia and commemorative documentation of a past generation's determination to remember their war.

Few collective experiences are richer in patriotic experience than armed conflicts. Wars cast long shadows. They establish and institutionalize personal and collective bonds, memories and symbols. They instill values and loyalties. Politicians and scholars have long seen war as a unifying force, especially in fragmented societies — an occasion to forge lasting memories and bonds of common experience.

Canadians know, too, that wars can be divisive and leave bitter memories that shape the behaviour and structure of civil communities long after the guns cease firing. The South African War demonstrates the validity of both claims. Among English Canadians the war reinforced a sense of community, of sharing common experiences, identity, symbols, attitudes and manners. Among French Canadians the war created a negative point of reference, one of exclusion, division, distrust and injury.

The South African War, 1899-1902, pitched an Empire that boasted possession of one-fifth of the world's surface and a quarter of its population, against the South African Republic and the Orange Free State, two small Afrikaner republics whose combined fighting forces numbered no more than fifty thousand men. While long-standing ethnic conflict and a more recent struggle over the exploitation of gold and diamonds had embittered relations between Afrikaans speakers and the largely English-speaking foreigners, strategic objectives, and European rivalry over the partition of Africa precipitated the intervention of British troops and subsequent military conflict.

Armed with the best rifles and artillery that their gold-rich country could procure from Germany and fighting on familiar ground, the Afrikaners or 'Boer' armed combatants initially outnumbered, outgunned and outmanoeuvred the more conventional and poorly led British forces. Even after the British gained an overwhelming numerical superiority, reorganized and revitalized their leadership and obtained formal control of the republics, the Boer's guerrilla tactics infused by their passionate defence of their homes and homeland made the 'formally' conquered republics ungovernable. The British military's desperate military tactics, their scorched-earth policy, their systematic confiscation of their opponents' livestock, the burning of their crops and farms and the herding of their women and children into concentration camps (where death rates from disease and malnutrition reached scandalous proportions) only fuelled the Boers' determination to resist, and to continue the struggle to its bitter end.

Canada's participation in the South African War was not automatic. A heated, sometimes hysterical public debate and a divisive, two-day Cabinet crisis preceded the government's capitulation to a strident pro-war lobby's demand that it authorize the recruitment of an initial one thousand citizen volunteers for service in South Africa, in defence of the imperial estate. In October 1899 an initial instalment of troops left Quebec City to participate in Canada's first military expedition abroad.

Before this war reached its bitter end on 31 May 1902, more than 7,368[1] adventurous young Canadians, officially between the ages of twenty-two and forty, (one was only fifteen and a large number were under twenty-two) served with the British forces in South Africa. Although most of Canada's troops served during the first, more conventional phase of the war, before the dirty war of farm burning and concentration camps began in earnest, even they joined in the early stages of this unfortunate strategy. Others, such as the Canadian constables in the South African Constabulary, the 2nd Canadian Mounted Rifles, and the Canadians in the small irregular 'British' units such as the Canadian Scouts, participated more fully in these distasteful activities.

Organized into eleven different units, many Canadian volunteers were re-enlisted veterans, men who rejoined another Canadian unit upon the expiration of their initial one-year service contract. Perhaps another three hundred Canadians joined irregular forces such as the Canadian Scouts. In addition, Canada sent twenty-three artificers, a sixty-four-person hospital unit, eighteen nursing sisters, twelve instructional officers, six chaplains and five postal clerks.

In battles at Paardeberg, Zand River, Mafeking, Diamond Hill, Liliefontein, Lydenberg, Harts River and elsewhere, Canada's citizen volunteers fought with tenacity, stamina, skill and courage. Their success became a source of pride to their compatriots, and their experience informed their country's response to the Great War. As many as thirty-four of the 106 generals in the Canadian Forces during the Great War were Boer War veterans, as were many other distinguished Canadian senior officers.

Canadians were proud of their soldiers' accomplishments. Civilians at home fought the war in oratory, prose, poetry and song, in print and on canvas. Children played soldiers. Civilians cheered their troops' departure, consumed war news, celebrated their soldiers' victories, organized extensive support systems, welcomed them warmly upon their return and commemorated their deeds in marble, stone, bronze and glass. Through solicitations, patriotic benefit concerts and other community activities, civilians raised impressive sums of money to fund these causes. Organizations such as the Imperial Order Daughters of the Empire, the Soldiers' Wives League, the Patriotic Fund and Canadian branches of British beneficiary and service organizations owe their founding impetus and development to the war. Towns, streets, objects, parks, monuments and memorials remain a visual testimony to Canadians' efforts to honour and perpetuate their memory.

Canadians participated in this war for a variety of personal and collective reasons, though it threatened no vital Canadian interest, provided no apparent gain and left a bitter legacy of disunity and resentment. Public persons and bodies appealed to loyalty, allegiance and imperial solidarity; some saw it as a moral crusade; others supported the war for more pragmatic reasons: political status, future security and markets. The volunteer soldiers themselves were moved by patriotism, restlessness, adventure, pressure from peers, family and community and material motives.

This book is about conflict at home and abroad, conflict against 'an enemy,' within Canadian units, between Canadian and Imperial troops, and at home. It concentrates more on the home front than one might expect, especially the relationship between the home front and the war front. It recounts in detail only three battles, Paardeberg, Liliefontein and Harts River, celebrated Canadian engagements that commanded the public's imagination and memory. Those who wish a more comprehensive discussion of Canadian military activities in South Africa may consult my *Painting the Map Red: Canada and the South African War, 1899-1902* (Montreal, 1993 and 1998).

This book draws upon a wealth of archival material that was generated by the war. And it has benefited from the assistance and support of many persons and institutions that I would like to acknowledge with gratitude. I would like to thank especially Mary McDaid, my secretary, Kristen Pederson-Chew, Lorimer's senior trade editor, and Pam, Danielle, Marc, Elin, Marius and Andrew Miller.

The visuals accompanying the text were assembled and selected by Lori McLellan of Lorimer. Thanks are due to the Canadian War Museum for their help in providing many of the items used.

—C.M.

1

THE WAR

Historians disagree on the war's causes, and the reasons for Canada's participation. Canada's post–World War I historians read Canadian participation in the South African War as the unfortunate outcome of a British conspiracy. Anxious to demonstrate Canada's political evolution from colony to nation, they regarded the South African War as an unfortunate precedent that retarded our evolution toward constitutional autonomy; a conflict that revealed the linguistic fault line of our history.

They focused their suspicions on several British officials. Their prime suspects were the British Colonial Secretary, Joseph Chamberlain, the Canadian Governor-General, Lord Minto and the General Officer Commanding the Canadian Militia, Major-General E.T.H. Hutton, who they accused of conspiring to force Canadian participation. Faced with the alternatives of sending troops or leaving office, the Liberal government of Sir Wilfrid Laurier had weakly capitulated. According to this historical construction, English Canadians had mindlessly rallied to the flag to defend

"The Twentieth Century belongs to Canada"

throne and altar, kith and kin, oblivious to French Canadian sensitivities and indifferent to the harm they were causing their country.[2] In short, this war was a precursor to the 1917 conscription crisis, and the result of an 'imperial conspiracy.'

In the 1950s, a scholar-librarian, H. Pearson Gundy,[3] exploded the myth that Canada's participation in the Boer War was the result of an imperial conspiracy. A decade later a historian, Carl Berger, redefined imperialism as another form of English Canadian nationalism.[4] Their radical reinterpretations of imperialism oblige historians to question the previous generation's conspiratorial construction of Canada's participation in the South African War. In fact, Canada's decision to send troops to South Africa was a form of home brew, a reluctant, politically motivated capitulation to the demands of Canada's pro-war advocates, not the clandestine machinations of a handful of imperial conspirators,[5] orchestrated from London.

During the last decades of the 19th century, some British politicians and activists attempted to reorganize the British Empire to provide greater economic, military and political security in an increasingly competitive and threatening international environment. The movement called itself imperialism, and cloaked a welter of conflicting and

Sir Wilfrid Laurier and his Cabinet

white man's war, label it a Boer or Anglo-Boer War — a dispute in which the large number of armed and non-armed Black participants become non-people, at best 'pawns in a white man's game.'[6] At the end of this so-called 'white man's war' there were more armed African combatants than there were Boer soldiers!

Those who see the war as a response to socio-economic imperatives — the machinations of international financial or strategic requirements, a piece in the larger European scramble for territory — prefer the designation South African War. This broader designation recognizes the central and complex role of Africans in the conflict. It acknowledges that Africans fought on both sides: as combatants and support; against one another; and for their own strategic objectives, though often patronized, marginalized and confined to menial duties. One recent author has perceptively concluded that perhaps the South African War was many wars, depending upon the participants and their objectives.[7]

self-serving motives and aspirations. It thrived on ambiguity. Although the Canadian branch of the movement possessed a purpose, program and character of its own, designed largely to secure the Canadian-American border, the movement's association with language, ethnic and religious issues made it anathema to French Canadians, who feared its centralizing grasp and culturally monolithic agenda.

During the heyday of journalism, no literate Canadian ought to have been surprised by the outbreak of war in South Africa on 11 October 1899. Months before Afrikaner troops moved into British territory, informed Canadians had read, discussed and debated the deteriorating relations between Britain and the two South African republics of the Transvaal (South African Republic) and the Orange Free State. As one might expect, historians have disagreed on the causes of the war.

A lively dispute over naming the war reflects historians' differing opinions. Was it a Boer War, an Anglo-Boer War, a second War of Independence or a South African War? Those who see it as an ethno-cultural conflict, or as a

Turn-of-the-century Toronto

The Boers

According to the ethno-cultural historians, the war was a clash of cultures, a contest of language, law and custom, whose roots began with the British purchase of the Dutch colony at the Cape of Good Hope following the defeat of Napoleon Bonaparte in 1815. The British purchase of this strategic post, designed to secure the sea lanes to their lucrative Indian empire, included a self-conscious community of French- and Dutch-speaking Protestants (Afrikaners or Boers) that had been settled at the Cape since the 17th century.

The ethno-cultural historians' tale begins in 1820 when the Boer (a Dutch word meaning farmer) community's homogeneity was challenged by the arrival of 4,000 British settlers to protect their Cape naval garrison, an act some historians feel initiated the subsequent clash of cultures. The clash continued in 1828 with the British decree that English be the official language of the colony, and in 1833 by their abolition of slavery, a measure that undermined the Boer economy, and precipitated a Boer exodus from the colony. The so-called 'Great Trek' became a defining moment, a historic reference of mythic and religious proportions for the Boer community.

The 'Great Trek' took place between 1834 and 1845, when about fourteen thousand Boers and their servants, over half of the colony's white population, left the Cape Colony and trekked northeast into the South African interior to escape British control and to relieve natural demographic pressures. There they constituted a buffer between the growing British coastal settlements and the Bantu peoples, the large African linguistic group including the powerful Zulus that occupied the interior lands. The British never recognized the Boer trekker's independence, and continued to view them as British subjects. In 1848 the Governor of Cape Colony, Sir Harry Smith, made this clear when he annexed all of the land from the Cape up to the Orange and Vaal Rivers and to the Drakenberg Mountains.

Renewed conflict between Boer and Briton accompanied the expanding British population's encroachment on the Boer trekkers' borders. Intermittent fighting forced Britain to recognize the Boer-trekker republics of the

Queen Victoria

Orange Free State (1852) and the Transvaal (1854). But sandwiched between the British and the Bantu, the Boers had difficulty maintaining their independence. During their 1876-77 confrontations with the Zulu, the Boers' depleted treasury and internal strife obliged them to accept British annexation in exchange for military and financial aid. This short-lived arrangement ended in 1880-81 when Paul Kruger, Piet Joubert and M.W. Pretorius led a successful revolt, the so-called First War of Independence, re-established self-government for the Transvaal and renamed it the South African Republic. The British government's loss of nerve, following their humiliating defeat at Majuba Hill, brought the first Anglo-Boer War or War of Independence to a conclusion. In the Pretoria (1881) and the London (1884) Conventions that

defined the Republic's autonomy, the British insistence upon the legal equality of Boer and British within the Republic became the source and pretext of future conflict. Those who see the war as the outcome of socio-economic determinants argue that the discovery of diamonds near the Vaal River and Harts River in 1867, and gold in 1885 on the Witwatersrand, almost sixty-five kilometres south of Pretoria, created the conditions for the subsequent armed conflict. These rich mineral deposits drew a tide of largely English-speaking foreigners into the Transvaal, aggressive miners and entrepreneurs who needed a compliant, sympathetic

Paul Kruger

state. To secure its compliance, they demanded the right to choose their rulers, more particularly the right to vote. Since the Boers believed that the Uitlanders [outsiders], as this group was called, constituted close to a majority of all male residents, their enfranchisement would entail the peaceful surrender of the Voortrekkers' republic, a condition to which its old President, Paul Kruger, would never consent.

An obsession with gold, diamonds and ethnic conflict, however, obscures the catalytic influence of strategic considerations in transforming a local dispute into an imperial crusade. Europe's late 19th century 'scramble for Africa,' to secure strategic advantage and checkmate their military and industrial rivals, took on a life of its own, frequently defying economic advantage.

After the discovery of gold, the British government had been alarmed by the shift of economic and strategic power from the British-controlled coast of southern Africa to an unpredictable Afrikaner-controlled interior that increasingly sought closer protective relations with Britain's European competitors. Germany's 1884 annexation of the territory between the Orange Free State and the Portuguese colony of Angola (Namibia), Kruger's purchase of German arms and armaments and Germany's subsequent diplomatic and military support of Kruger's government gave the dispute an international character. In the end, strategic considerations probably triggered the armed conflict.

Whatever the cause, lines were soon firmly drawn. The more extreme Boers, who remembered their 'expulsion' from the Cape, talked loosely of reclaiming the Cape, and 'driving the British into the sea.' The more extreme British imperialists talked just as recklessly of extending British influence and control from the 'Cape to Cairo.'

Children's game featuring Paul Kruger

A standoff seemed inevitable.

When insurrection, agitation, petition and negotiation failed to secure Uitlander 'rights,' the British government responded to its stridently imperialistic press's call for action by reinforcing the weak British military presence in South Africa; at once a show of force and a security precaution. Paul Kruger, seeing that the arrival of British troops would diminish his military advantage, issued an ultimatum. He demanded that the British government withdraw its forces from the Transvaal borders within forty-eight hours, recall those that had landed since June or were on the high seas, submit their grievances to international arbitration or face war. Early on the morning of 11 October 1899, Boer troops moved into British territory.

Troops on parade

2

The War of Words

Well before the first shots were fired, Canadians were engaged in a civil war of words on the wisdom and necessity of Canadian support of British arms in South Africa. A heterogeneous coalition of pro-war advocates, composed of influential progressives, pragmatists and party politicians with strong ties to the urban press, clamoured for Canadian participation in the war. The diversity, rationale and equivocations of this loose pro-war coalition, however, were drowned out by the rhetorical excesses of a fanatical few.

On the eve of a federal election, several aggressive, large, urban, English-language dailies attempted to stampede public opinion and embarrass a sensitive Liberal government into sending troops. The fanatical few were led by Hugh Graham, the owner and editor of the Montreal *Star*, a nominally 'independent' jour-

British lions on the march

nal with close ties to the Conservative party. According to Graham, Canada's decision to send troops was nothing short of a victory of the fourth estate.

Graham's journal, whose unscrupulous tactics have been described as 'unique in Canadian journalistic history,'[8] led the crusade, ably assisted by the Toronto *Telegram*, the Toronto *Mail and Empire* and the Hamilton *Spectator*. Their verbal abuse and hysteria embarrassed many of their pro-war colleagues, whose opponents tarred them with the same brush.

Their primary tactic was to vilify the Boers, romanticize the Uitlanders and infuse the imperial crusade with a missionary, progressive urgency and zeal. Neither their message nor their method were original. Both were borrowed from abroad, though frequently they bore a local colour or construction. Sensational headlines, fabricated stories, incendiary editorials, carefully selected letters to the editor, poems and cartoons portrayed the Uitlanders as oppressed servants of empire besieged by a crafty, cruel and dishonest Boer people, in league with a foreign, hostile power determined to destroy the last vestiges of British influence in South Africa. The cause was personalized; and opponents, real and perceived, were pilloried and abused.

Front-page stories 'amply verified' told of Boers dynamiting trainloads of fleeing women and children and kicking to death the secretary of the South African League; tales tailored to create a sense of outrage and the impetus for immediate action. One headline read 'Boers Act Like Untamed Savages,' and related how Boers had spat in the faces of English women, shouted obscenities and defiled the water at railway stations, stories guaranteed to shock Victorian sensibilities and create a 'thrill of horror.' More sensational charges claimed that the Boers, in preparation for the war, were advertising for two real Bushmen to make their famed poison. 'The named above poison,' the alleged advertisement read, 'must be suitable for soaking our bullets, as, I think, it would be very unfortunate that our enemies should be shot with bullets not so soaked.'

Both the cause and its chief protagonist, the Transvaal's President, Paul Kruger, were barbarized. Kruger, a simple, accessible, God-fearing republican who wore a plain green sash as his only insignia of office, was pictured as a dictatorial autocrat attired in imperial garb surrounded by timid, compliant sycophants. Alternately they portrayed him as a crude, crafty peasant who drank four gallons of beer a day (guaranteed to offend the strong Canadian temperance lobby) and ruled over a horde of degenerate, black veldt farmers, corrupted by Uitlander wealth.

What distinguished the *Star* and its fanatical allies from many of their pro-war colleagues was their reduction of the contingent debate to a contest of wills between French and English Canadians. They blamed French Canadians for the government's initial reluctance to commit Canadian troops, especially as other British colonies were doing so. In their language, French Canadians, 'an insignificant' minority, were holding hostage the English Canadian majority. Meanwhile cowardly English Canadian cabinet ministers submitted meekly to their dictates. According to the Montreal *Star*, Canada was being humiliated in the eyes of the Empire and

HIS "PRECEDENT" BOGY WON'T SCARE.

TARTE—"I fix dis up beautiful, zen I make Bourassa run away from eet, zen I pretend me t have great fright, but ze people pass by and sing 'God Save ze Queen,' and say I make ze grand fon of myself—Sapre!"

Israel Tarte in political cartoon of the time

bartering away its claims to security, prestige and material benefits. Canada, the popular British poet Rudyard Kipling's "Lady of the Snows," had lost its opportunity to volunteer first for battle.

The French Canadian Prime Minister became the butt of their verbal abuse. They portrayed Laurier as a weak, vacillating man, an eloquent, polished but facile grandee, ready to celebrate the Queen's Diamond Jubilee in 1897 (the Tory press never recovered from Sir Wilfrid Laurier's extraordinary popularity in London on that occasion), but the last to offer material assistance to Britain in a time of need.

The fanatical press cast Laurier as a hopelessly malleable, spineless man, manipulated by his wily Minister of Public

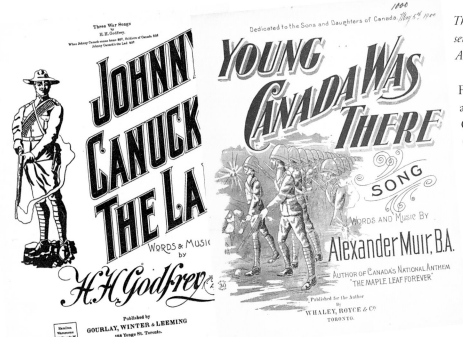

Patriotic sheet music

The Canadian contingent was
sent COD,
A disgrace to our land.

Feelings ran high and the verbal abuse became outrageous. French Canadians were dismissed as Canadian Boers, who lived in a priest-ridden, backward community "honeycombed with traitors and conspirators who had been granted 'lingual and religious privileges that never should have been granted.'"[10]

"It is time Sir," wrote one prominent Toronto physician, "to wake up in this country to the fact that we may have questions to settle which may not be set to rest by the ballot."[11] Hysteria reached such levels that the Governor-General, Lord Minto, reported that Eastern Ontario farmers went to bed with guns, fearing a French Canadian assault. And John Charlton, a leading businessman and increasingly embittered Ontario Liberal Member of Parliament, openly advocated stationing troops in Quebec City![12]

Although the overwhelming majority of vocal French Canadians rejected a Canadian military involvement in clear, unmistakable language, French Canadians' response to the war was less monolithic and tribal than their more hysterical opponents imagined.

While not one French Canadian journal — Liberal, Conservative, independent, religious, recreational or commercial — advocated sending a Canadian contingent to South Africa, a few prominent individuals, such as the Mayor of Montreal, Raymond Préfontaine, actively supported the British, and a small, articulate group of French Canadians supported the Boer cause. Most simply remained indifferent, preoccupied by more immediate practical concerns.

None saw the material necessity of supporting the world's greatest military power, while British preoccupation in South Africa exposed Canada to the danger of an American attack,

Works, Israel Tarte, 'Master' of Laurier's administration. Tarte offered an ideal target for Conservative wrath. Irreverent, irrepressible and a renegade Conservative, Tarte had helped deliver Conservative Quebec to Laurier's Liberals in 1896. Cartoons represented Tarte as speaking a broken English with a heavy European French accent. "When British women and children are being murdered wholesale by the Boers," wrote the Hamilton *Spectator*, "it is high time that the Boers' friend Tarte was out of the government of a loyal British Colony."[9] Students, townsmen and even a Toronto-based militia company, the less literate of whom believed him to be one of Kruger's generals, burned the unpopular minister in effigy. Others knew precisely what they were doing as they chanted their fiery refrain:

We'll burn Tarte and Laurier
On a black birch tree;
They're traitors to Canada,
Not worthy of MP

especially along the tenuous Alaskan boundary. In these circumstances, Canada might better retain its troops at home to protect its part of the imperial estate. Sending Canadian troops to South Africa seemed a needless tax on Canadian resources more usefully employed at home.

Even more alarming, if not sinister for French Canadians, were the anticipated constitutional implications. Generally, they viewed colonial wars as dubious adventures promoted and designed by imperialists to consolidate the Empire, and represented in Canada by the Imperial Federation League and other organizations, including the Orange Order, with its program of 'One School, One Flag, and One Language.'

Many French Canadians feared the movement's constitutional and political agenda. In their view, imperialism threatened to dismantle the liberal, colonial settlement based on self-government, liberty and diversity — characteristics that had defined Canadian constitutional development. They saw war as a prelude to imperial integration and centralization, a backward step in Canada's political evolution. They suspected that the imperialists' real agenda was the subordination of all British possessions to a central authority in London, maintained by military force and supported by a blood tax on colonial men and resources, levied without representation and consultation.

Perhaps most of all, French Canadians feared imperialism's cultural agenda. Despite its leadership's best efforts,[13] the Canadian imperialist movement had become synonymous with unilingualism, militant Protestantism and majoritarianism, so forcefully associated with D'Alton McCarthy, the sometime president of the Canadian Federation League and the man who led the attack on French Canadian linguistic

War coverage in the French-Canadian press

and educational rights outside Quebec.

A small number of French Canadians openly identified with the Boers, a minority like themselves trying to preserve their identity against the corrosive influence of an alien culture. Some drew fanciful historic parallels. They compared their colonization of the Lac St. Jean area to the Boer's Great Trek, and the Canadian Rebellion of 1837 to the First War of Independence. They lauded their common 'Latin' origins, their agrarian life, their patriarchal families, their simple manners, their deep piety, their courage, determination and passion for liberty.

Illustrations in some French Canadian journals depicted Boer women and children rallying loyally to the defence of their homes and their country, sharing their men's adversity, and choosing death rather than surrender. "Qui sait," one journal asked, "si un jour la pomme de discorde ne viendra pas des rives du Saint Laurent?"[14] Had French Canadians chosen which army to join, the small Ottawa liberal daily, *Le Temps*, concluded, many would have chosen "l'armée commandée par les Joubert, les Cronje, les Viljoen."[15] One perceptive contemporary observer wrote that French Canadians "saw a race, not English, about to be brought into subjection by the whole force of the Empire and suffer the loss of their race ideals. Apprehension can easily draw parallels."[16]

Similarly, behind the apparent linguistic monolith lay a more diverse and subtle English Canadian reality. Above all, the English Canadian response was more than a tribal response to the claims of blood and belonging; or an occasion to abuse French Canadians. During the conflict, Toronto's former Oxford don, Goldwin Smith, shrewdly observed that

Toronto was "the centre of jingoism and almost its circumference."[17] Although an overstatement even if he had included English Montreal, he was correct in reminding us that jingoism was less prevalent in small town and rural Ontario and Quebec than in the large cities. Similarly western Canadian and Maritime papers, Liberal, Conservative and Independent, tended to dismiss the 'racial' agitation as an eastern or central Canadian problem and to condemn it as dangerous, disloyal and disruptive of the war effort. Unfortunately, these discordant responses have escaped the notice of many historians, too dependent on the accessible, entertaining vignettes found in the large urban dailies.

They ignore the small, well-defined but ineffective English Canadian opposition to the war among farmers, radical

Romantic depiction of Boer patriots

labour, Protestant clergy and anglophobic Canadians of German and Irish descent. This loose and disparate opposition based its dissidence upon a broad range of liberal, socialist, pacifist and practical objections, including the war's cost and inhumanity, and its violation of the constitution and Christian principle.

Most of the anti-war farm journalists were classical liberals, opposed to imperialism, big government, standing armies and taxation. They regarded participation in this war as an invitation to empire, a costly precedent. Like their French Canadian compatriots they deplored throwing away "life or treasure in the African wilderness," when both were urgently needed at home to develop the Canadian West.[18] They fre-

quently identified with the Boers, whom they described as sober, God-fearing, brave and unyielding, not the "race of uncultivated and incorrigible savages" depicted by the yellow press. In their view, the Boers were pioneers like themselves, a "poor pastoral people" courageously "fighting under a grim old Kruger, who trusts God and keeps his powder dry." They noted the irony of the Boers worshipping "the same God we profess and follow and who are pleading the righteousness of their cause at his feet," — an irony not lost on some of the Canadian officers during the war.[19]

Radical labour journalists who opposed the war shared the farm journals' concerns with the war's cost, its wastage of men and resources, its constitutional implications and the growth of a military establishment. They espoused a romantic sympathy for Kruger, that "fine old man," and his "little Boer republic" with its pious, courageous, pioneering people, that had tamed a wild country and whose bullets "have sung the song of desperate resistance."[20] They saw war as the natural outcome of capitalist greed and exploitation, and imperialism as its crudely fashioned cloak. More radical journals condemned volunteers as "curs," who "left their families in destitute circumstances" to "bayonet human beings for 40 cents a day and the chance to get a piece of metal with V.C. stamped on it,"[21] and they called upon soldiers and workmen to refuse to fight, to "Stop The War And Arrest The Murderers," to use the slogan of one handbill circulated by Montreal trade unionists. They

E HATH HER VICTORIES NO LESS RENOWNED THAN WAR."

Henri Julien's caricature of Laurier

ridiculed the government efforts to boom "the cemetery business in Boerland."[22]

Radical labour's anti-war journals, however, were not all of one mind. The Kootenay mining journals, the *New Denver Ledger*, and the *Sandon Paystreak*, sneered at the Christian Socialism of the *Citizen and Country* or the Winnipeg *Voice*, and their concern for what Christ thought of imperialism or what Jesus might have done. God, the *New Denver Ledger* sarcastically thundered, was "always on the side that had the most men and the greatest number of guns."[23]

Although Canada's anti-war Christian Socialists regretted that the "Army of the Prince of Peace is divided,"[24] they were proud that a small number of clergy and laity in most Protestant denominations risked the wrath of their congregations and condemned the war.[25] A few, such as the Maritime Baptists' *Messenger and Visitor*, appeared to possess a distinct sympathy for the Boers, applauding their courage and condemning the immorality of the war.[26]

Moreover, before the war broke out, religious journals provided only tepid support for the conflict. In fact, the Presbyterian *Record* and the *Westminster*, and for a time the

Christian Guardian, the voice of Canadian Methodism, attempted to dampen the more extreme vitriol. Even the Toronto-based *Canadian Churchman*, the Church of England's family paper, prided itself in having "countenanced no jingoism" and prayed to the last that "England may be spared a war which…cannot but bring in its train consequences so disastrous and so dishonouring."[27] A greater ambiguity stalked the columns of the *Canadian Congregationalist*. It prayed that "Canadians…[who were] called upon to serve in South Africa may never stain their hands with the blood of their fellow man."[28]

Moreover, Canadian historians have paid little attention to an amorphous body of moderate, reasoned opinion, indifferent to ideology, and far from convinced of the need for Canadian participation. During the pre-war debate, the Ottawa *Journal*, the Montreal *Witness*, the Quebec *Telegraph*, the Hamilton *Herald*, the Sherbrooke *Record* and even Toronto's fashionable *Saturday Night* called for no volunteers, and saw no reason for Canada to rush troops to the Transvaal.

Furthermore, during the pre-war debate on Canada's role in the war, the partisan Liberal press remained remarkably disciplined and united behind its leader's ambivalent 'wait and see' stance. They rebuked their Tory competitors for their "gilt-edged loyalty," dismissed their ranting as the work of a syndicate of liars, and called for calm and deliberation. Some partisan Liberal journals, such as the Sarnia *Observer* and the Moncton *Transcript*, were so opposed to Canadian participation in the war that even after the government's decision to authorize the dispatch of troops they took some time to rally to the war cause.

Many influential anglophone public figures, such as Oliver Mowat, the former Premier of Ontario and George M.

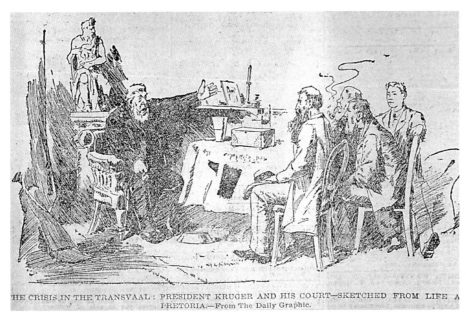

HE CRISIS IN THE TRANSVAAL : PRESIDENT KRUGER AND HIS COURT—SKETCHED FROM LIFE A
PRETORIA.—From The Daily Graphic.

Paul Kruger represented as a dictatorial ruler

and political interests in the war. In their view, war was an opportunity to rid their country of its colonial status, forge a mature relationship with Britain, gain a greater voice in imperial councils and obtain international recognition. Many described it in gendered language as a manly bloodletting initiation rite, a test of manhood, to secure a place in the community of nations. It was also an opportunity to repay Britain the estimated $55 million it had spent on British North American defence — less a repayment than a premium designed to purchase Britain's protection of Canada's territorial claims along the tenuous Alaskan panhandle following the failure of the International Joint High Commissions.[29] In short, Canadian participation was the modest price of membership in the imperial defence club.

Grant, the influential Principal of Queens University, were profoundly embarrassed by the 'racial' fanaticism of some of their pro-war colleagues. Unlike the fanatical few, they advanced pragmatic and ideological reasons for Canadian participation.

Some journalists, clergy and politicians justified Canadian participation in moral, ideological terms. They saw the war as a loyalty test, a question of imperial solidarity, of allegiance to a common Queen, flag, kith, kin, language and governance. Many prominent progressives, such as Salem Bland, the Social Gospel advocate, Agnes Maud Machar, the poet, J.W. Bengough, the popular cartoonist and J.J. Kelso, the child saver, saw the conflict in South Africa as a struggle between civilization and barbarism. Convinced that Canada had a moral obligation to 'Christianize' and 'civilize' the world in 'our generation,' they were prepared to compel the "decadent and medieval" nations of the world to conform to "the canons of civilization." In this struggle, Canadian soldiers were merely "missionaries togged in khaki, Bibles at the end of guns." "Civilisation Advances" is how the Victoria *Colonist* greeted the outbreak of war.

Other pro-war advocates insisted upon Canada's material

Others identified more material motives, such as the opportunity to attractive lucrative war contracts and war profits. "Canada has strong commercial reasons for seeing British ideas prevail in South Africa," wrote one Canadian pamphleteer, and enumerated the Canadian products that might find a profitable market in South Africa.[30] Backed by their government, many Canadian merchants followed his advice and sent representatives to South Africa. During the war, the British War Office spent some $7.5 million in Canada on horses, materials, food and fodder.

English Canada's response to the outbreak of war in South Africa, therefore, was more than a tribal, ethno-linguistic contest of wills. While some English Canadians opposed participation, many worried about the justice of the cause, its constitutional implications and its cost. Many were indifferent. Others advocated Canadian participation for political and economic reasons.

Similarly, the French Canadian response to the war was more complex than simply an anglophobic reflex, a response

Recruits for the first contingent, some in uniforms, some in civilian dress

motivated by blood and belonging. As Jean-Guy Pelletier pointed out several decades ago, French Canadian war opponents represented a wide spectrum of social, political and cultural concerns.[31] Consequently the extent, intensity and durability of French Canadian opposition ought not to be distorted. While no francophone journal advocated Canadian participation in the war, once the Canadian government had committed Canada to sending troops, the large dailies such as *Le Journal*, *La Presse*, *Le Soleil*, and *La Patrie* accepted the *fait accompli*. Moreover, after the severe British defeats of Black Week (10-17 December, 1899), others such as Jules-Paul Tardivel's *La Verité*, worried about the nefarious consequences of a British defeat in South Africa on Canadian security on this continent.

These subtleties were of little assistance to Canada's beleaguered Prime Minister, the recently knighted Sir Wilfrid Laurier. Pressurized by an increasingly clamorous and virulent press debate, Laurier's efforts to avoid antagonizing English Canadian sensibilities on the eve of a general election were increasingly threatened by the focused intensity of the fanatical few.

3

THE CANADIAN CONTINGENT CRISIS

The outbreak of war in South Africa riveted public attention on Laurier's divided Cabinet. How would the country's first French Canadian Prime Minister negotiate the treacherous waters of public opinion? On the eve of a federal election, and far too sensitive to his ethnic and religious vulnerability, Laurier had sought to enhance his electoral support, especially in central Canada's urban centres, where the party remained weak but support for the war was strongest.

Confident to the last that war would be avoided, Laurier discouraged hopes that the government would send an official contingent. If British security were at risk, there was no question that Canada would assist. But he (and the Conservative Sir John A. Macdonald before him) saw no reason for Canada to participate "in all the secondary wars in which England is always engaged."[32] He denied the existence of any Canadian military preparation, doubted its necessity,

worried about its costs and questioned Canada's constitutional right to send troops abroad. To relieve public pressure on his government, Laurier encouraged private offers of assistance. In short, he tried to hold "a block of ice to the back of Canada's neck."[33]

Laurier's diversionary tactics fooled few. Moreover, the outbreak of war shattered his strategy and gave him little space to manoeuvre. The question now was to send or not to send troops, and if so, upon what conditions.

Laurier felt the mounting pressure, as the fanatical pro-war press became more strident, insistent and menacing. Independent journals such as the Ottawa *Journal*, while rejecting the extremist language of the fanatical few, began to waiver and call for a token offer of assistance. Dangerous fissures began to develop within his party's ranks. Toronto's leading Liberal paper, the *Globe*, threatened to join the chorus calling for a token offer. Its defection would lead inevitably to other defections, particularly in urban centres where the Liberal Party was most vulnerable and where public meetings were turning into loyalist demonstrations.

Reasonable, influential friends and supporters such as Principal Grant and George T. Denison, the avid Canadian imperialist, now pressed Laurier for action. Moderate non-partisan bodies such as the Canadian Club of Toronto, joined the growing call for Canadian troops. The Montreal Corn Exchange interrupted its proceedings to intone patriotic refrains. Rumours of large public meetings being planned in Hamilton, Toronto and Montreal seemed more ominous still, especially in Montreal, where a demonstration might degenerate into a physical confrontation between French and English. Meanwhile two influential, absent cabinet colleagues, David Mills and Louis Davies, urged Laurier to send troops, as did the Canadian High Commissioner to the United Kingdom, the powerful Lord Strathcona. And Laurier's Minister of Militia, Frederick Borden, assured the *Globe* that Canada was prepared to send troops. He only needed a Cabinet decision.

Nevertheless war seemed to take Laurier by surprise. In fact, so confident had he been that war would be averted that he had left Ottawa for Chicago to participate in an international ceremony surrounding the opening of a post office building. Upon his return, Laurier learned at the London, Ontario station stop that hostilities had begun. As the train

CANADIANS IN KHAKI
South Africa 1899 - 1900

OFFICIAL CORRESPONDENCE
NOMINAL ROLL CASUALTIES ETC
PRICE 25 CENTS

moved toward Toronto, he became "very sober and silent." John Willison, the editor of the *Globe* and his travelling companion and confidant, pleaded with Laurier for an immediate, positive decision. In Willison's opinion, Laurier had little choice. He "would either send troops or go out of office." When they parted at Toronto, however, the Prime Minister remained "reluctant, unconvinced and rebellious."[34] The news got worse when Laurier reached Montreal and his masterful Minister of Public Works, Israel Tarte, opposed to Canadian participation in the war, met him with tales of public protest meetings and growing French Canadian resistance.

Meanwhile, imperial presumption and conspiracy theories had complicated a difficult situation. Just before Laurier had left for Chicago, the British Colonial Secretary, Joseph Chamberlain, had sent a generic telegram to all self-governing colonies thanking them for their generous offers of troops and indicating the organizational form their assistance might take: company size, and infantry units of about 125 men that could be integrated easily into British battalions. The Deputy Minister of Militia, Colonel L.J. Pinault, had inadvertently released the telegram to the press and it created a furor. Who had offered Canadian troops and by what authority: the Canadian government? The Governor-General? The General Officer Commanding (GOC) the Canadian Militia? Or was this merely an imperial tactic to force the Canadian government's hand?

No sooner had Laurier denied that his government had offered troops or had any plans to do so, than the *Military Gazette*, a journal in the confidence of the GOC, contradicted the Prime Minister. It informed the public that indeed the government had plans to send an official Canadian contingent of some 1,200 men, composed of infantry, cavalry and artillery. The information was correct. During the previous summer a plan had been devised, with the knowledge and consent of the Minister of Militia. The plan's existence had been conveyed to the British War Office through the Governor-General, Lord Minto, a close personal friend and apologist of the abrasive GOC, Major-General E.T.H. Hutton.

All of this looked suspiciously like an orchestrated imperial conspiracy to force Canada to send troops. Since Laurier had left for Chicago before he had untangled this web of misunderstanding, in his absence, the Acting Prime Minister, the crusty and irascible old Irish Canadian Minister of State, Sir Richard Scott, sought answers from the Governor-General and the Major General. Their resistance to his accusatory inquiries convinced Scott of their complicity.

The day after Laurier returned to Ottawa, he convened his divided Cabinet to determine Canada's response. The meetings lasted for two days, from noon until 5:00 p.m., the key players leaving occasionally to consult colleagues and partisans. There were three factions within the Cabinet. Tarte

Colonel Otter, seated, centre, surrounded by his staff and two Canadian nurses

and Scott opposed sending an official Canadian contingent. They objected to its cost and the lack of consultation and parliamentary approval, and were convinced that Minto, Hutton and Chamberlain had conspired to force Canadian participation.

Opposed to Scott and Tarte were the Minister of Militia, Dr. Frederick Borden, and the Postmaster-General, William Mulock, the wealthy leader of the Ontario caucus. In their view Canada could send nothing less than an official contingent, recruited, equipped, transported and paid by the government. Both ministers saw participation in the war as an opportunity to enhance Canada's status within the Empire, and enter the community of nations; in the words of Borden, it was an occasion to announce to the world that Canada was no longer a colony but a "mature nation of the empire."[35] To achieve this objective Canada must send a force worthy of Britain's senior Dominion, a full battalion, under senior Canadian officers, not small company-sized units that would be absorbed into British battalions. Since plans for the dispatch of a government-sponsored contingent were now public knowledge, anything less would be political suicide, at least in Ontario.

The Militia Department's plan had called for a balanced force composed of one battalion of infantry, a squadron of cavalry and a battery of field artillery, altogether a unit of 1,209 men, 314 horses and six field guns, the nucleus of what military planners affectionately called "Canada's little Army in the field." Lieutenant-Colonel Lawrence Buchan was tagged to command the infantry, Lieutenant-Colonel François-Louis Lessard the cavalry, and Lieutenant-Colonel Charles W. Drury the artillery. As more troops were sent this balanced skeleton force would expand and be kept together. The entire unit was to be commanded by Lieutenant-Colonel William Dillon Otter. Quite apart from the aid Canada's little Army might render British arms, their battle experience would be invaluable experience in reforming the Canadian militia.

Between these extreme positions, a middle group led by two powerful cabinet ministers, W.S. Fielding, the Minister of Finance and Clifford Sifton, the Minister of the Interior advocated a limited liability strategy. They suggested restricting Canada's contribution to the modest demands of Chamberlain's offending telegram.

The first day, Cabinet decided nothing, except to reconvene. According to the anxious Governor-General, Tarte and Scott seemed to have carried the day with their charges of imperial complicity. But when the Cabinet reassembled the following day, the centre of gravity had shifted. Rumours of public demonstrations, telegrams from influential friends and supporters and the wavering opinion of the partisan and independent press had taken its toll. Shortly into the second day, tensions reached a breaking point, and Mulock stormed from the Cabinet, seemingly never to return.

Laurier realized that he could temporize no longer. Sensitive to his perceived liabilities of "race and religion," during his first mandate he had pursued a charm strategy in English Canada, especially in Ontario. His imperial preferential trade policy, his flattering reception in London during Queen Victoria's Diamond Jubilee, his knighthood and his settlement of the contentious Manitoba schools controversy had won him a wide popularity in English Canada that he hoped to translate into votes. The defection of a key Ontario cabinet minister on an imperial issue would have seriously damaged his electoral strategy. A compromise had to be negotiated quickly.

As soon as Cabinet approved a conveniently ambiguous agreement, Laurier left for Rideau Hall to inform the Governor General that Canada would send troops. Fielding, a former journalist and editor, and advocate of the middle way, communicated the government's decision to the press. The government would recruit and equip "not more than 1,000 infantry volunteers," divided into eight companies of 125 men each. They would be transported, paid, maintained and returned to Canada at the expense of the British government. Fielding explained to the press that the Canadian government's modest expenditure of public funds required to recruit the troops, was "under no circumstances to be regarded as a departure from the well-known principles of constitutional practice, nor construed as a precedent for future action."[36]

On the face of it, the government's 'limited liability' had all the appearances of a carefully constructed compromise with no clear victors. Eight companies of infantry were but a 'token' contribution, a far cry from Borden and Mulock's balanced Canadian contingent of all arms. Its modest dimensions conformed faithfully to Chamberlain's earlier

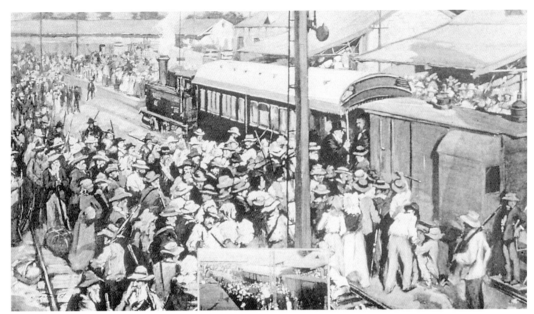

request. Its Canadian cost was limited to its recruitment, an administrative expense not sufficiently significant to require Parliamentary approval; after this the British would pay the bill. This was far from the 'blood tax' feared by its opponents. The 'no precedent' clause was the price of the opponent's consent, especially French Canadians' well-founded fears that it was only a first instalment, a justification for participation in future colonial wars.

Laurier stretched credulity to maintain the fiction. In Ontario he insisted that his government's response had been constrained by Chamberlain's telegram, instructions that were part of the British War Office's plans that applied to all colonies "without exception."[37] To Quebec, he dismissed the government's decision as a harmless formula to permit English Canadians to join the British Army. Henri Bourassa, the brilliant young Liberal Member of Parliament, who Laurier had marked for a Cabinet post before he resigned his seat in the Commons to protest the government's decision to send troops, was not deceived. A student and admirer of British constitutional law and practice, he realized that the precedent was the "fait accompli." He was right. The contingent was but the first instalment of a much larger consignment of

Canadian troops for South Africa; more than six thousand would follow the 'gallant thousand' over the course of the next thirty-two months.

Clearly, the government had agreed to send troops not because it was the hapless victim of imperial threats, conspiracies and machinations, but because it feared electoral defeat.

4

THE CANADIAN CONTINGENT

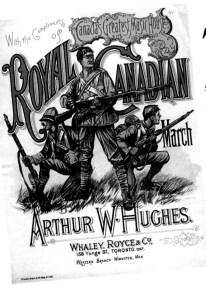

Musical tribute to Royal Canadians

The Prime Minister's fiction was short-lived. Laurier had scarcely finished justifying Canada's limited military liability when the Cabinet made an offer 'more worthy and representative' of Canada's size and place within the Empire. Few were happy with the government's decision to organize the men into small, independent, company-sized units that might be broken up and integrated into British units. Conscious of the public's desire to make the contingent a national statement, Borden organized the companies into two battalions, four companies to a battalion, under Canadian officers and made every effort to give it a distinctive character within the British family.

Determined to enhance the contingent's importance, extend its autonomy and affirm its national character, Borden designated it the 2nd Battalion, The Royal Canadian Regiment of Infantry, making it an extension of its namesake of the Permanent Militia. This association underlined the fact that the volunteers were not British Army recruits, but men with a temporary appointment in Canada's Permanent Militia. Canadian officers led the battalion; the pro-war press had made that a condition. The battalion's Commanding Officer, Lieutenant-Colonel William Otter, reported to both the British military authorities in the field and the Canadian military authorities in Ottawa.

The battalion organizational structure required senior Canadian officers, a regimental structure and auxiliary staff including two adjutants, a quartermaster, a transport officer and a paymaster, and permitted the addition of three chaplains (Church of England, Methodist and Catholic), two medical officers (one anglophone and one francophone), a historical recorder and instructional officers. The most popular chaplain was the kind, fearless and tireless bilingual Father Peter O'Leary: "Say, I am a Protestant," wrote one of the

Troops take a rest

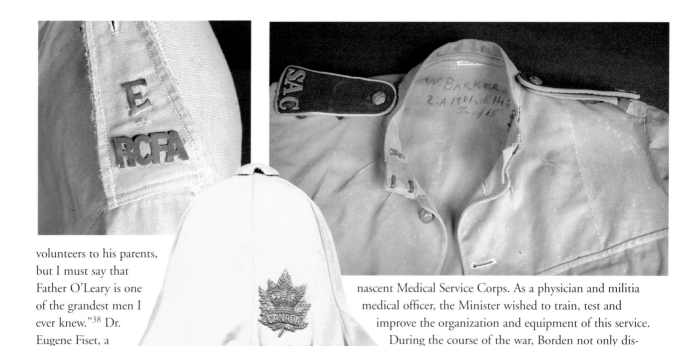

volunteers to his parents, but I must say that Father O'Leary is one of the grandest men I ever knew."[38] Dr. Eugene Fiset, a future Lieutenant-Governor of Quebec, was almost as popular among the men. Four newspaper correspondents, a YMCA representative and a Red Cross officer accompanied the unit, though they were not officially attached to Canada's first contingent.

Borden used the war to test and legitimate Canada's

nascent Medical Service Corps. As a physician and militia medical officer, the Minister wished to train, test and improve the organization and equipment of this service.

During the course of the war, Borden not only dispatched Canadian nursing sisters to South Africa, he dispatched a full-fledged field hospital.

Four nurses accompanied Canada's first contingent. Since no provision had been made for medical services in the original organization, Borden offered their services to the British military authorities. The British accepted the offer, but discouraged sending more than those required for Canadian troops as "British law permitted only doctors registered in the

Distinctive uniforms of the Canadian Contingent

United Kingdom and nurses in the British Army Reserve to care for British troops," a ludicrous provision in light of the subsequent chronic need for competent medical assistance.

To give the first contingent a representative regional and linguistic character, recruitment offices were opened in the principal cities and towns across Canada. Recruits were organized into eight regionally defined companies, from the Pacific to the Atlantic, identified by letters from A to H, each company numbering 125 men. A Company contained all the volunteers from British Columbia, the Northwest Territories and Manitoba; B Company was raised in southwestern Ontario; C Company was the Toronto company; D Company included the recruits from Ottawa and Kingston; E was the Montreal company, while F Company was reserved for all the francophone recruits and led by bilingual officers and non-commissioned officers; the men in G Company came from Saint John and Charlottetown; and H Company was the Nova Scotia unit, recruited largely in Halifax and Amherst.

The battalion's Canadian character was reinforced by material distinctions. The Royal Canadians' brown canvas khaki uniforms, white helmets (later sensibly dyed coffee), heavy black boots, Sam Browne belts and Canadian-invented Oliver equipment — as well as their small distinctions of dress and kit and insignia — underlined their desire to differentiate themselves within the imperial family. No distinction provided greater pride than the maple leaf 'Canada' badge affixed to their helmets. Subsequent units possessed comparable distinctions in name, dress and equipment.

Recruiters sought males between the ages of twenty-two and forty years of age, with a minimum height of five feet, six inches (two inches taller than required in the British Army), who could pass a standard military medical test. Men with military experience were the most sought after, preferably infantry rather than artillery or cavalry. Their service contract was for a year or the termination of the war, whichever came first.

The response was overwhelming, especially among urban blue- and white-collar workers. The first contingent contained thirty-one university students, eleven teachers, two medical doctors, thirteen lawyers, four dentists and twelve professional engineers, as well as the sons of notables. Militia officers reduced their rank to enlist as privates. In Nelson, British

Columbia, only eight men were chosen from seventy applicants; in Vancouver, seventeen men were retained from sixty volunteers, and so it went. Men jostled and contrived to secure a place. Deception and influence were rife. Men lied about their age, family friends interceded, sympathetic militia doctors overlooked physical disabilities and political influence altered decisions — though it was less rampant than many believed.

Many volunteers were disappointed, especially those in the cavalry and artillery. Among them was the artillery officer John McCrae, the future author of *In Flanders Fields*. "It is all over!" he wrote despondently after the dispatch of the first contingent. "I see by tonight's bulletin boards that there is to be no second contingent. I feel sick with disappointment. I do not think I have ever been so disappointed in my life — for ever since this business began, I am certain there has been no fifteen minutes of my waking hours that it has not been in my mind: this is no exaggeration. My position here I don't count as an old boot beside it; nor anything else much, as I think now." He was to get his chance.

What moved men like McCrae and others to volunteer for military service in this distant conflict? Contemporary Canadians answered this question on both a public and a private level. Educationalists, journalists, clergy and politicians promoted participation in the war as a moral and ideological crusade, affirmations that historians have replicated. In their view Canada's gallant thousand volunteers, and the more than six thousand compatriots who followed them, were a mirror reflection of Canadian society, "the pick of the nation's sinew and brain," the "representatives of ideal Canadian manhood," a 'true' image of their country.

Contemporaries were no less categorical in identifying the volunteers' motives. In their view these "Lords of the Northland," "pure as the air of the sunlit North," responded to the claims of religion, blood, right, glory, progress and freedom, selflessly determined to "fight and bleed for the world's great need." In short they were secular missionaries of sorts, in an era of missions.[39] The reality is somewhat different.

In fact, the volunteers were far from representative of Canadian society, even of Canadian male society. The men who populated Canada's contingents were largely young, single, anglophone, urban workers drawn from the low-paid, blue-collar and service sectors of the country's urban society, at a time when 68% of Canada's population of five million lived in rural areas. Only 3% of the volunteers were French Canadians, whereas French Canadians accounted for some 30% of the country's population.

About 30% of all Canadian volunteers were British-born; in some units, such as the Strathcona Horse, as many as 50% were British-born — at a time when the British-born accounted for only 7% of Canada's population. Some 40% were members or adherents of the Church of England, whereas this denomination represented no more than 12% of the Canadian population.[40] At least 16% of all Canadian recruits came from low-paid clerical occupations — they were clerks, grocers and bookkeepers, occupations that represented only 2.9% of Canada's male workforce.[41] Blue-collar workers, carpenters, machinists, painters, plumbers, blacksmiths and electricians made up most of the rest.

The contingent's social composition varied from unit to unit, depending upon the time and place of their recruitment. Units recruited in western Canada contained large numbers of British-born cowboys, ranchers, farm labourers, packers, prospectors and policemen. Representative of Canadian society they were not; nor were their motives so obvious and singular as public rhetoric might suggest.

Ideology may have moved some men to volunteer. After all, many were the products of a first generation of state-supported, compulsory education, a literate community increasingly vulnerable to the printed word and the era's ideological fashions. And no contemporary movement seemed more compelling than British imperialism, including its particular Canadian variant, an amorphous movement that cloaked a variety of conflicting and self-serving motives and aspirations.

Committed to building a strong and healthy nation, a greater Canada within a united Empire, imperialism was promoted by the school, the press, Protestant churches and a growing number of patriotic and civic voluntary organizations such as the Sons of Canada, the Sons of England, the Sons of Scotland, the Boys Brigade, Cadet Corps and the Navy League. Increasingly, public school curricula inculcated patriotism and loyalty, discipline and leadership, reinforced by school drills, demonstrations, exercises and patriotic anniversaries; some were freshly minted, such as Empire Day and Queenstown Heights Day. In this era of missions and missionaries, in many Protestant churches, the flag, the 'open' Bible and the English language seemed as indivisible as the Trinity — and young men were urged to join missionary crusades to rid their own land of evil and win the world for Christ in their generation.

A popular literature fired young men's imaginations and desire for adventure and travel — especially to defend their imperial estate, which covered a fifth of the world's surface and on which the sun never set. Many recruits revelled in stories of manly adventure, endurance, heroism and empire building found in the popular writings of Rudyard Kipling, G.A. Henty, Robert Michael Ballantyne and H. Rider Haggard, and juvenile journals such as *Chums* and the *Boys Own Journal*. Walter Bapty, who volunteered for service in three Canadian units, recalled that as a child he tried "to emulate the heroes of the Henty and Ballantyne books by cooking out of doors, sleeping in tents and building fires."[42] Another recruit, Edwin McCormack, who served in the second contingent, often imagined himself one of the Johannesburg boys in Henty's *With Buller in Natal*.[43]

Others were fascinated by the contemporary American invasion of Cuba, a war the American yellow press depicted as a noble crusade of instant heroes. A number of Canada's South African volunteers were veterans of that conflict. Many underestimated the war's duration and seriousness. Confident of the might and power of the Empire against the apparent weakness of its foe, some saw the South African War as a gigantic picnic, a poorly contested 'march to Pretoria,' where everyone would eat Christmas dinner before returning to the praise and gratitude of their compatriots.

Subtle and cohesive social pressures from family, chums and community also persuaded men to volunteer. The number of sons of prominent citizens represented more than patronage and influence; for many public persons it became a loyalty test. Few parents emulated Mrs. Barry, who exhorted her son to defend the Empire as her father and grandfather had done. When Cecil Barry died during the Battle of Paardeberg, the family sent another to replace him. Altogether three Barry sons served in the war!

Peer pressure and friendship served as another powerful recruitment tool. The number of men who joined with their school, sports, militia and work chums or their brothers (there were forty-three sets of brothers in the first contingent) demonstrates the social dynamics of recruitment as well as the importance of fraternity in warfare.[44] Many others were "pals at home and belonging to the same baseball clubs."[45] The Ottawa Rough Riders sent at least five of their best men. Fred W. Coombs, a 24-year-old, Prince Edward Island–born clerk who worked in Saint John and was twice captain of the city's renowned Mohawk hockey team served as a corporal in G Company with four of his teammates. Few seem to have been drawn from their homes by the single call of throne, language, race and religion.

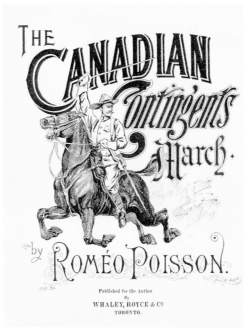

Inspired by the war

Choosing and fielding the men for Canada's first overseas contingent was the most visible challenge to the country's inexperienced, rudimentary and underfunded military establishment; and they would only receive public notice if they failed. Volunteers had to be enrolled, clothed, equipped, housed, and collected from the cities, towns and villages where they had been recruited and brought to the port of embarkation within two and a half weeks of the government's decision to send troops.

The Minister of Militia, Dr. Borden, a man of almost inexhaustible energy, led by example, working long into the night and on weekends. Together, Canada's often-maligned public service, citizen militia and small professional military establishment assembled a credible field force. Thanks to their industry and dedication, and without employing one additional clerk, a 1,039-man, relatively self-sufficient, semi-autonomous Canadian militia unit was ready to leave Quebec City one day before the War Office's deadline of 31 October. They were truly public servants, committed to the welfare of their country and its citizen army.

The Canadian Contingent

5

THE PUBLIC'S WAR

The Canadian public support for their contingent was never in question. They mobilized immediately to fete, honour and support their soldier heroes. Once the government announced its decision, all but a small, disparate number of the ideologically opposed joined the civilian crusade.

Toy soldiers styled after the Canadian Contingent

rate demonstrations were organized, replete with parades, triumphal arches, bands, banquets and interminable speeches by politicians, clergy and local notables. Cheering crowds lined streets decorated with flags, bunting and patriotic slogans. Many civic leaders' popular decision to grant their employees a holiday swelled the noisy crowds.

Public enthusiasm was infectious, especially in urban centres. It claimed the energy, time, resources and imagination of all sectors of society, irrespective of class, age or gender. Newspapers hailed the men as patriots; clergy, politicians and public persons praised their courage and sense of Christian duty; poets sang their praises. No language seemed too exaggerated. Friends, family, voluntary organizations, patriotic and fraternal organizations, militia units and civic communities feted their soldiers' departure and showered them with compliments, advice, gifts and comforts.

At various concentration centres across the country, elabo-

As the men made their way toward Quebec City, the port of embarkation for the first contingent (all the rest left from Halifax), small groups gathered at railway stations to cheer, secure souvenirs, give speeches and serenade the soldiers with patriotic songs. Even "in the dead of night," a Kamloops paper reported, "stirring British cheers awoke the mountains and rivers telling the tale of brave British hearts passing along to defend the honour and glory of the old Flag." In the Ottawa Valley at each station stop "farmers were lined up with Snider rifles and saluted as the train came in."[46]

Although impressive public ceremonies marked the departure of all ten of Canada's South Africa contingents, none rivalled Quebec City's farewell for the Royal Canadians. To mark the departure of Canada's first expeditionary force abroad, official Ottawa, from the Governor-General down to senior civil servants, descended on Quebec, a city whose population was no more than seventy thousand persons in 1901. They were joined by some ten thousand visitors, relatives and friends. Accommodation was so scarce that some soldiers were reportedly billeted in houses of ill repute; their presence in brothels may not have been the fault of the military authorities!

Public enthusiasm for the war inspired the music

Impressive church parades, one Protestant and the other Catholic, preceded the final secular ceremonies. At the Protestant service, held in the Church of England's Holy Trinity Cathedral, President Kruger himself could not have made more skillful use of scripture and liturgy to incite the men to "Stand Up for Jesus," "Fight the Good Fight," and uphold "the charter of the world's freedom" once given to the Israelites but "now in England's keeping." The Catholic service was somewhat tamer, a low mass celebrated by the battalion's Catholic chaplain, Peter O'Leary.

During the departure ceremony the next day on the Esplanade, not far from the monuments to Montcalm and Wolfe, the secular rhetoric resonated patriotic duty, meaning and admonition. The men were hailed as makers of Canadian history, comparable to Jacques Cartier, Champlain, Montcalm and Wolfe, and those who had repulsed the Americans in 1775, the War of 1812 and the Fenian raids, and defended Canadian integrity the Northwest Rebellion;

and now were enjoined to carry "the banner of civilization into the very heart of Africa." In the words of some, their service affirmed Canada's indissoluble unity and maturity; it announced to the world that they were no longer a colony but a mature nation of the Empire. After all the rhetoric, those who had enlisted for personal or material reasons might have found it difficult not to believe themselves heroes and patriots.

Many of the "gallant thousand," as several speakers branded them, may have been too tired to heed the moralizing rhetoric. They had been in full battle gear, a weight of seventy-five pounds, since 8:00 a.m., awaiting orders to begin their march through the old town to the Allan Wharf, where the *Sardinian* waited to transport them to South Africa. It was with a visible relief that they finally received orders to march through the narrow, winding streets and cheering crowds, led by the bands of Montreal's 5th Royal Scots and Quebec's garrison of Royal Artillery. At about 3:30 p.m. the ship left the wharf and the Citadel's guns fired a thirty-one gun salute. The combined bands played "God Save the Queen," followed by the shriek of sirens, ship's whistles and rockets fired from the *Sardinian*. No volunteer crowding the deck of the old *Sardinian* could have failed to be impressed by the crowd's enthusiasm, gratitude and support.

Aboard the overstuffed *Sardinian*, tangible evidence of the country's support abounded. No gift was more popular than tobacco, a manly product suitable for a soldier! Not only had the men received predictable, large consignments of tobacco from the American Tobacco Company and J. Davis & Sons, but the Montreal Soldiers' Wives League had donated twenty thousand cigarettes, one thousand pipes and over six thousand pounds of tobacco. Some people lamented that there was "so much tobacco and so few Bibles."

Devotional materials, however, were not lacking. The Quebec Bible Society, the Watford Bible Society and the Soldiers' Wives League contributed a sufficient number of Bibles, in French and English, to provide one for each volunteer. In addition, the Methodist Book and Publishing House sent 150 volumes of patriotic and religious literature. Boxing gloves "in sufficient number to stock a prizefighter's gymnasium," a harmonium, whiskey, and over two hundred cases of unspecified comforts, including delicacies, games and books, testified to the public's determination to support their men at the front.

Well before the government's decision to send troops, the public began mobilizing civilian resources for the men and their dependents. Many employers granted volunteers leave, some with pay. Volunteer organizations remitted membership fees during a volunteer's absence. Others insured their members' lives and made provisions for the care for their dependants. Hugh Graham, the imperialist editor of the Montreal *Star,* with a steady eye on a British title, saw the war as an opportunity to ingratiate himself with the British authorities. Well before the war began, he made arrangements to purchase a one-million-dollar insurance policy from the Ocean, Accident and Guarantee Company for the men of the first contingent, at a cost of twenty thousand dollars. Similarly, individuals and municipalities purchased policies against death and wounds in combat for their men.

Almost every city, town or village set up patriotic funds, sponsored receptions, and provided comforts and cash gifts for local volunteers. On average, each private received about twenty-five dollars from his municipality; those who collected more gave the rest to their company commanders to spend on comforts; some company officers simply divided the sum

Guards Have Gone to War and Taken the Hearts of Their Countrywomen With

Sentimental views of war

among the men rather than engage in the invidious task of buying for some and not for others. Considerable sums were collected. For example, Saint John's Transvaal Committee raised $28,294; Hamilton collected ten thousand dollars; and Montreal obtained seven thousand dollars during the first week of its campaign. Moreover, Canadians contributed generously to many imperial charitable war-relief funds, including the Widows and Orphans Fund, the Officers' Life Insurance Fund, the Soldiers of the Queen Relief Fund, the Mansion House Fund and the Absent Minded Beggars Fund.

No group proved to be more committed home-front soldiers than women, if one can judge by their rhetoric, rhyme, benevolence and willingness to volunteer for war service. As propagandists, memorializers and writers,[47] they expressed their pro-war sentiments in unmistakable language, much of it reprinted in the Reverend J.D. Borthwick's *Songs and Poems of the South African War.* Women incited men privately and publicly to volunteer, lauded their patriotism and sought patriotic meaning and moral purpose in their deaths and injuries, often in aggressive language. "Onward Christian Soldiers," wrote Dorothy Coutts as a tribute to Harold Borden. "Spill your blood for your ideas. The precious drops thereof will, like the blood of the martyrs, become the seed of generations that will redeem the effete morality of your time."[48] Nor were women reticent to volunteer for the limited 'front line' service available to them at the time as nurses and teachers.

Women were instrumental in collecting public, corporate and private funds to aid their men at the front. The recently founded Imperial Order of the Daughters of the Empire vied with the newly organized Canadian branch of the Soldiers' Wives League and the National Council of Women to raise monies for comforts. Women worked in various war charities, including the Red Cross, and the Canadian Patriotic Fund.

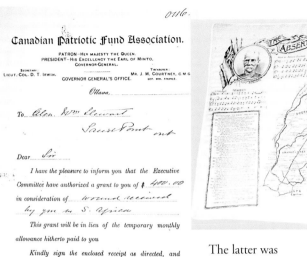

Raising money for the war effort and patriotic songs were fashionable

The latter was founded by the Governor-General, Lord Minto, and collected some $340,000 to care for disabled soldiers and their dependants.

While many of these funds were led by an elite and secured large donations from banks, insurance companies, railways and municipalities, other charities raised monies from ordinary people and through more modest means such as chain letters, auctions, the sale of patriotic songs and poems, and, most popular of all, a patriotic concert.

Patriotic concerts enabled local communities to express their commitment and contribute to the coffers of war charities. At Seaforth, Ontario, an interdenominational religious concert in January 1900 at Cardno Hall raised $117 for the Red Cross Fund. The following month, a concert in the booming gold town of Dawson City netted $1,320 for the Absent Minded Beggars Fund. In Ottawa, a recital sponsored by the British *Daily Mail* under viceregal patronage raised an impressive five thousand dollars. Patriotic concerts became so popular that they soon attracted entertainment entrepreneurs who demonstrated their faith in profitable patriotism by pocketing half the profits!

Children joined the civilian crusade, contributing to a variety of community and school projects. The most celebrated was the Montreal *Star's* (Hugh Graham again!) "Children's Testimonial to Queen Victoria and Patriotic Fund for Families of British Soldiers in the South African Campaign," which raised $16,547.17 in denominations of five cents to a dollar. The money was sent directly to Queen Victoria, accompanied by an illustrated address and a 250-pound album containing the photographs of the thousand children who had contributed.

Two days after the Canadian government announced the dispatch of troops for South Africa, Dr. G. Sterling Ryerson, a strident advocate of Canadian participation, created a Red Cross Fund to provide comforts for the men in the field. Under the patronage of the Governor-General, and with the assistance of the National Council of Women, the Red Cross Fund collected some thirty thousand dollars, over seven thousand dollars for food, medicine, tobacco, boots and clothing, and provided "grants of money to men left in various hospitals."[49] In addition to the collection of funds, about fifty boxes of "clothing, medical supplies and condensed milk" were shipped to Quebec, valued at over fifteen thousand dollars. Not content to raise money and ship goods, Dr. Ryerson accompanied the second contingent with a fifty thousand-dollar line of credit, to visit men in hospitals and supervise the distribution of comforts.

The YMCA's presence in Canadian militia camps was established well before Confederation. Their tents offered recreational substitutes to wet canteens and an evangelical alternative or supplement to the military's more conventional religious establishment. So ubiquitous had the YMCA become in military camps that Dr. H.G Barrie's accompaniment of the Royal Canadians created little difficulty. Aboard ship, Barrie organized variety concerts, prayer meetings and evangelical religious services each Sunday evening. In South Africa, he visited the sick, distributed comforts, reading and writing materials and facilitated communications with men and their friends and families.

A relentless company of willing civilians and civilian organizations assisted in innumerable ways. Churches continued to

Christmas postcard from South Africa

became the fashionable colour, including khaki-coloured handkerchiefs in silk with flags embroidered in the corner, and Soldiers of the Queen suspenders in khaki sold by the Dominion Suspender Company. The Toronto Lithographing Company and J.C Wilson of Montreal produced a series of Boer War postcards, including Wilson's Soldiers of the Queen series, similar to W.J. Gage's earlier Soldiers of Canada series, which featured photos of some of Canada's senior officers, such as William Otter, François Lessard, Oscar Pelletier, Sam Steele, Lawrence Buchan, Thomas Evans, Charles Drury and Laurence Herchmer. Few businesses fared better than the insurance companies. Their services were in high demand, sometimes insuring men three times over, but restricting benefits paid for death or battle wounds.

provide rhetorical support and consolation for the bereaved. On Sunday, 11 February 1900 the Canadian churches organized a day of prayer for the men, ironically the day the Royal Canadians began their march to Bloemfontein, and a week before the bloody first battle of Paardeberg.[50] Individuals dispatched an enormous number of food packages and maintained a voluminous correspondence. Letters to and from men from the same communities enjoyed a wider circulation at home and at the front.

Those who had anticipated a profitable war were not disappointed, nor were people averse to exploiting opportunities. Retailers did a brisk business akin to the Christmas market as friends, relatives and organizations rushed to purchase gifts, supplies and comforts for the men. Merchants offered discounts on goods purchased for soldiers and employed military themes to sell anything from diamonds, wristwatches — "the convenient way for military officers and men to carry the time," books, maps, buttons, calendars and commemorative plates to Dr. William's Pink Pills for Pale People or Dr. Chase's Ointment used by the men of the first contingent.

Fashion assumed military hues. Few Christmas novelties, the *Monetary Times* reported in December 1900, "failed to introduce in some part or other of their composition, a bit of Johnny Canuck or Tommy Atkins." Khaki

Handkerchief with patriotic themes

6

BOREDOM OF WAR

The excitement, elation and romanticism of warfare faded slowly aboard the *Sardinian*. Thirty days' confinement to its congested quarters proved a brutal foretaste of the boredom, monotony and regimentation of warfare. As the old *Sardinian* made its slow, rolling progress toward Cape Town, personal feuds and regional rivalries developed that pursued the battalion to South Africa. The men's grievances focused on their conscientious but ineffective Commanding Officer, a good staff officer who many dismissed as an insensitive martinet.

Built to accommodate about seven hundred men, the *Sardinian* carried a consignment of 1,061, including two stowaways from the Quebec garrison, four nursing sisters, four newspaper correspondents and a ship's crew, together with their equipment, horses, several dogs and a month's food and provisions. Toilet facilities were inadequate; medical supplies were deficient; the fruit supply was insufficient; lifeboats were too few; and water was so scarce that a guard had to be posted over the tap. The Lower deck was overheated and claustrophobic. The Upper deck was so blocked by baggage that it was difficult to move about. Men ate and slept in the same area, consigned to hammocks or cots that were so close that they were within reach of one another, in quarters where the stench of food mingled with fresh paint and seasickness.

A semblance of order soon replaced the initial confusion of embarkation and four days of seasickness. Otter immediately instituted a strict military regime, convinced that his men and officers lacked military experience, discipline, drill, and musketry practice, and a knowledge of military duties and interior economy. Conscious of his colonial status and anxious to appear professional and create a favourable impression upon

Postcard home from a weary soldier

Men embarking

The S.S. Sardinian

to their military inactivity in South Africa. They blamed him for his tardy investigation of the exorbitant prices of the ship's canteen, typed him as a mindless anglophile and held him accountable for every imperial stupidity. They complained of his indifference to their physical conditions and accused him of favouring the Toronto company. They never forgot his thoughtless order when they reached the tropics that the men go about barefooted and with "their trousers rolled up to their knees, the idea being to harden the feet."[53] The result was severe sunburn.

Despite the troop ship's constraints and the military routine and discipline, there was time for recreation and various antics. Sometimes life took on the air of a schoolboy's excursion. It began with the "bath under the salt water hose the first thing in the morning," and included evening entertainment, reading, writing, playing cards,

his British superiors, Otter conformed strictly and often needlessly to British military regulations.

Otter's obsession for copying "all the wrinkles of the British regiments" irritated his men and officers.[51] Men resented his 'petty edicts,' the excessive saluting and rigid insistence that hundreds of men sitting or lying about come to attention every time an officer appeared. In a citizen force where personal and family friendships transcended rank, and where no clear social distinction separated the commissioned and non-commissioned ranks, Otter's excessive insistence upon deference to distinctions and proper salutation seemed forced and artificial. Men later learned with perverse pleasure that British troop ships normally dispensed with saluting! Otter's ceaseless fussing over form, protocol and appearance earned him a number of names, including "the Old Woman."[52] He never managed to secure the confidence of his officers and men.

All too soon, Otter became the scapegoat for all the men's grievances, from the physical conditions aboard the *Sardinian*

boxing or gambling. Although proscribed by military law, Albert Perkins, a young Fredericton boy witnessed "one fellow lose $29.75 [equivalent to a month's pay] in a few minutes," while another won over one hundred dollars in gold.[54] Dr. Barrie offered alternate entertainment, a prayer meeting, followed by an impromptu concert of instrumental music, songs, mimicry and skits, ending with the hymn "For Those in Peril on the Sea." Nevertheless after thirty days aboard the *Sardinian*, all cheered the sight of land.

The Royal Canadians had no reason to doubt the warmth of Cape Town's welcome on 29 November 1899. Greeted by ships' sirens and whistles, as soon as the *Sardinian* docked an

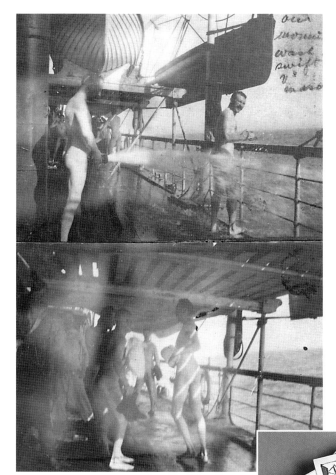

Salt-water bath aboard ship: the most enjoyable event of the day

spending a subject of commentary in the local papers.

When their train left Cape Town the next day, thirty-five of the men were absent without leave; they had lost their kit or were too drunk to move. The rest, led by a pipe and bugle band, marched to the train station through massive, cheering crowds. At the station, Lord Milner and the City Mayor addressed the men before they boarded the slow-moving, narrow-gauge train for their forty-four hour journey through the Great Karoo, along the single-track railway toward De Aar.

The Canadians' dispatch was deceptive. After four days at De Aar, the "Dust Bin of Creation,"[55] they moved to the Orange River Station, and then to Belmont, the rearguard of the British Army in Cape Colony. Here they remained — except for C Company's brief excursion to Sunnyside on New Year's 1900 — for the next two months, restless, bored and disgruntled, their only battle being against disease.

A paralyzing confusion and uncertainty faced the Royal Canadians upon their arrival in South Africa. The first phase of the War had ended in mid-December with three major British defeats at Stormberg, Magersfontein and Colenso. These defeats were known by the British as "Black Week." During this period, the war had been fought on British territory, in the northern and central Cape Colony and northwestern Natal, a battle in which the British were outnumbered, outgunned, badly mounted, without proper maps and generally poorly prepared for Boer warfare. The Boers, whom the yellow press had dismissed as ignorant, dull peasants, were skilled marksmen and tacticians armed with modern weaponry, who could more than hold their own against the British.

Forbidden by military law, gaming was rife

official delegation came aboard to welcome the Canadians. A demonstrative public welcome awaited them the next morning as they made their way through streets of noisy spectators toward their campground at Green Point Common. More welcome still was the news of their immediate departure the next morning for the front. Meanwhile, the thousand or so ship-bound, happy warriors descended upon Cape Town's restaurants, theatres, brothels and places of amusement, with a month's pay in their pockets, their prolific

Shaken by these unexpected and humiliating defeats, the British rearmed, reorganized and restructured their strategy

Lord Roberts, and music dedicated to him below

and higher command. Lord Frederick Roberts came out of retirement to replace Sir Redvers Buller ("Reverse Buller," as his critics unkindly called him) as Commander-in-Chief, ably assisted by Lord Herbert Kitchener, the energetic, exacting, forty-nine-year-old hero of the Battle of Khartoum who eventually succeeded Roberts as Commander-in-Chief in South Africa.

New leadership brought a new strategy, one of classical simplicity. Buller's war on three fronts with the object of encircling the Boers had turned into an expensive defensive operation. In contrast, Roberts and Kitchener decided to strike directly at the Boers' capitals, forcing them to withdraw their troops from other fronts, free besieged British fortresses and defend their seats of government. Above all, Roberts sought to engage the Boers in a decisive battle that would end the war, a strategy based on European assumptions about warfare. The novelty of the new British plan lay in its decision to follow the single-gauge rail line to Kimberly, and march men, transport and supplies overland, across unbroken plain, to Bloemfontein, the capital of the Orange Free State, moving from watering hole to watering hole.

The new strategy, however, required time to plan, organize and secure the necessary resources. Meanwhile career officers, anxious for place and preferment, manoeuvred for advantage, which left Otter sidetracked, increasingly immersed in the regimental administration that he enjoyed to a fault. His men, occupying a ringside seat, watched and wondered as troops passed to and from the front, leaving them to guard (and chat with) Boer prisoners, protect the railway, bury the dead, round up stray cattle and serve on outpost, duties that might have been performed by anyone. Discouraged by the British defeats and their conversations with the wounded coming down the line, men began to regret that they had volunteered. Others, including some of Otter's officers, secured employment with more active units.

Bored and disgruntled, the men vegetated at Belmont, and complained about the lice, the flies, the sandstorms, the dirt and the weather. They grumbled about the food, "the sour bread, bad coffee and tea and water rations."[56] And since the food always seemed insufficient, men spent their own money to supplement their meagre fare, purchasing food at exorbitant prices at local markets because Otter refused to permit a regimental canteen with the mistaken belief that it violated army rules. His only answer to the men's discontent seemed to be more regimentation, inspections, drills, target practice, fatigue, route marches, picket and outpost duty, all in monotonous succession. So discouraged were men with life at Belmont that one advised his mother: "If the boys took my advice, they would stay at home for there is nothing here but the burning sun and desert storms, in fact it is the most forsaken country I have ever seen."[57]

Nothing was more corrosive to morale than illness. Although most men suffered from dysentery at one time or other, enteric or typhoid fever was the 'deadly' plague of sedentary camps in South Africa and especially so during the early summer months of January and February. An intestinal infection caused by *salmonella typosa* and accompanied by a high fever, back and thigh pains, dysentery, vomiting and occasionally delirium and coma, this deadly disease plagued the Royal Canadians for months and was responsible for more deaths than Boer bullets. In the end, one-third of the men contracted the disease at one time or other. Recovery left men weak and disabled for months, confined to hospitals and separated from their chums.

Men in hospitals were appalled by the experience of being treated according to their rank rather than their disease.

Hospitals were often unsanitary, the food was poor, and the orderlies were untrained, rough, careless and often dishonest. Conditions were so bad that men tried to care for their chums rather than see them consigned to a hospital. As the disease made its way through the camp, men experienced feelings of helplessness, desperation and futility.

The men's apprehensions and discontent expressed itself in fighting and disorder. More men were court martialled for drunkenness, looting, insubordination, sleeping on duty and other irregularities in their two months at Belmont than in all the rest of the campaign. Looting was common, especially for food.

Offences reported to the Commanding Officer received stiff sentences. Men objected to the severity of his punishments. They felt they were often excessive and degrading. They also resented what they regarded as a double standard: offences committed by men were punished, while those by officers were tolerated. On one occasion, a company officer caught with a lamb persuaded

Soldiers await action

Otter that he wanted it as a mascot. Thereafter they changed their mascot whenever possible.

Otter, of course, was not the heartless, insensitive monster of his men's imaginations. He worried and fretted about their welfare, the 'villainous' water, the appalling medical services, the high casualty rates, his men's lack of proper clothing and accommodation, and he did what he thought reasonable to alleviate their distress. But he lacked the confidence to assert himself, to demand better fare, for fear his British superiors would consider his intervention amateurish and unprofessional. Above all, he failed to communicate his concerns to his men, and he appeared resentful and suspicious of those officers who attempted to ameliorate their conditions. He became increasingly isolated from all but a small coterie of his staff. Otter "will get roasted when the Boys get a chance I can tell you," Private Albert Perkins wrote his mother as early as January 1900.[58] Otter would pay a heavy price for his failure.

7

THE EMPIRE'S HEROES

The Royal Canadians' discontent and boredom ended abruptly on 8 February 1900. On that day Roberts appeared at Belmont and announced that the Canadians would join his long-awaited march to Bloemfontein. They were to be assigned to his 19th Brigade of Infantry, along with the 1st Gordon Highlanders, the 2nd King's Own Shropshire Light Infantry and the 2nd Duke of Cornwall's Light Infantry, all under the command of General Horace Smith-Dorrien, a popular, ambitious and skilful manager of men. Within three weeks the loyal Canadians were to participate in two celebrated engagements, both at Paardeberg, from which they were to emerge as the Empire's heroes.

Queen Victoria's scarf

As they stored their baggage on 11 February and prepared to leave Belmont, few Royal Canadians realized that it would be many months before they would enjoy the comfort of another tent. Clad in stiff, chafing khaki and ill-fitting shoes and carrying a rifle, bayonet and a forty-pound kit that included a greatcoat, the men trudged over dusty veldt in temperatures ranging

Banquets and medals honour the Canadian Contingent

between 100 and 114 degrees Fahrenheit. This punishing ordeal was made more intolerable by the commissariat's thoughtless lunch menu of salt pork and dry biscuits, and its failure to provide adequate water rations. Often caught in the rearguard behind a creaking caravan of slow-moving, overloaded transports, constantly stopping and starting and breaking down, the Royal Canadians were part of a noisy, cumbersome procession of some thirty-seven thousand men, fourteen thousand horses and twenty-two thousand mules snaking its course across the veldt during the hottest month of the year. The procession averaged eighteen to twenty miles a day, often at night when it was cooler, though dark, and the way covered in boulders, thorns and termite mounds.

Almost a week's relentless march brought the British to Paardeberg Drift on the banks of the

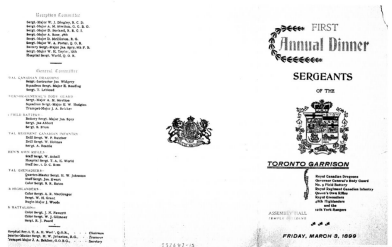

Boers had concealed themselves at the far end of the crook among the trees and shrubs along the river's bank. Instead of seeking the protection of the vegetation and natural trenches along its eroded river banks, the Canadians chose the most direct route to confront their opponent, across the somewhat undulated plain. Their only protection was the broken ground and a few blind, uncomfortable and insecure termite mounds, some as high as three feet.

About a mile from their crossing, the Canadians drew fire, though they were still well outside the Boers' range; the Boer's Mauser rifles had a range of some sixteen hundred yards.

Modder River. Across the swollen river was the Boer's legendary General Piet Cronje with some four thousand combatants and their dependants, entrenched along the river's banks, and determined to block the British advance on Bloemfontein, the capital of the Orange Free State. In the absence of Roberts, who was ill, and contrary to the advice of some of his senior officers, the impetuous Kitchener ordered his troops to storm the Boer positions.

According to orders, the Canadians were to cross the Modder River and prepare for action. The river formed a three-mile crook between them and the Boer positions. The

Extending the interval between the men from two to seven paces, the Canadians moved forward another two hundred yards or more before seeking shelter from the Boers' sweeping rifle fire. The Canadians returned fire, but inflicted little damage on their opponents securely shielded behind trees, shrubs and the river's bank.

During the next hour or more the Canadians tried desperately to move forward in short rushes, ten to thirty paces at a time. When rushes became too hazardous, they crawled on their bellies. The uneven pace of the movement made it difficult to keep the men together, and the reserve line and the firing lines became mixed up. Some men, however, came to within four hundred yards of the Boer trenches when they were stopped. Already they had gone too far, and they were pinned.

Modder River crossing

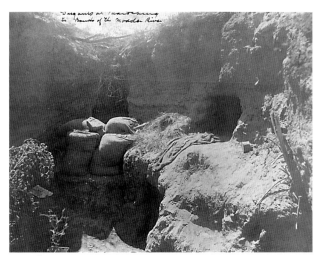

Boer dugouts

Canadians had failed to achieve their objective because of slowness, lack of experience, courage or leadership — despite the fact that the British Regulars had fared little better.

His terse interview with Otter ended, Aldworth sent one of his companies forward to the firing lines. In twenty minutes, two other companies followed, each time drawing enemy fire. Then at 5:15 p.m. he ordered his men to charge, offering "five pounds to the first man in the enemy trenches," and calling on the Canadians to join his suicidal assault. The Canadians responded to the bugler's charge with cheers and 'wild excitement.' John Todd, a British Columbia–born private who had been in the Spanish-American war, yelled out "Come on, boys; this beats Manila hollow," rushed forward and was shot dead, one of the many victims of the Boers' response. Aldworth and his adjutant were killed, as were many others, all for the temporary possession of two hundred yards.

Although the recall was sounded, few men could move. More exposed and vulnerable than before, they remained where they were, clinging tenaciously to the ground for whatever protection it offered. Without food and drink, all they could do was wait for the cover of darkness and endure the cries of the dying and wounded. "It was a night I will never forget," wrote Private William Campbell Warren, "to hear the groans and cries of the men on the battlefield." Men tried to assist their comrades. Richard Rowland Thompson, a twenty-two-year-old medical student from Ottawa, ran to aid his

For the next five hours the men sweltered in the scorching sun, the target of incredibly accurate Boer rifle fire, severe at times, then relatively slack. Suddenly in the early afternoon, the weather changed. An icy-cold rainstorm drenched the men and left them shivering. Then the scorching sun returned with its accompanying misery. Overcome by exhaustion, some men slept. Neither the ammunition carriers nor the stretcher-bearers, however, had that option. All day long they pursued their grim mission, driving their mules from the rear to the front lines, the target of Boer fire.

Otter was distraught. Twice he considered ordering an attack but thought better, fearing the great loss of life. Once he went in search of Smith-Dorrien. Failing to find him, Otter returned to the lines, tensely awaiting relief or directions. Then at about 4:00 p.m., Otter's cruel vigil ended.

Lieutenant-Colonel William Aldworth, the excitable British Regular commanding the Duke of Cornwall's Light Infantry, confronted Otter and curtly informed him "that he had been sent to finish the business and proposed going in with the bayonet."[59]

Aldworth may have been upset by his own battalion's relative idleness, or the implied rebuke of Kitchener's reassignment, or by some other temporary disorder. Whatever the cause, he demanded information on the disposition of the Canadian and enemy troops, insinuating that the

The heat of battle

friend, Private J.L. Bradshaw, who had been shot in the throat. Although Thompson was exposed to enemy fire, he lay alongside Bradshaw for seven hours, his fingers compressing Bradshaw's jugular vein to prevent him from bleeding to death.

Dr. Fiset moved relentlessly amongst the wounded and dying, administering aid and directing the overworked stretcher-bearers. The "little French doctor" became something of a hero to the men. According to one of his admirers, the reason "the death rate from fever and wounds had been so low among the Canadians is due largely to his unflagging zeal."[60]

Father O'Leary was no less courageous or revered by the men. All day this small, sympathetic priest comforted the dying, prayed for the dead, and provided first aid, water and cigarettes to the injured. According to one man, O'Leary "was better than a doctor to some of the men," kind, fearless and tireless. The evening before the battle he insisted on marching "with the rank and file…instead of going back to the transport." Although "his face and lips were swollen and he seemed about played out," when the men pressed him to ride in the transport wagon he just said that what was good enough for the men was good enough for him.[61]

Once darkness fell and the fire abated, Otter ordered his men back to the main drift for food and rest, and the Boers withdrew to their laager, about two miles up river. Meanwhile search parties and stretcher-bearers scoured the ground for the dead and wounded. Some of the officers and men joined the stretcher-bearers, to search for their friends and the men of their company. All night long the men stumbled through the dark, groping over the ground, their "hands steeped in blood," guided by the faint moans and "pitiful pleadings for water." Occasionally the searchers "would come upon a cluster of wounded closely huddled together…[who] unable to drag themselves from the field had come to each other for mutual companionship."[62] The injured were carried back to the drift; the dead were interred in a common grave nearby,

THE ANNIVERSARY OF MAJUBA HILL.

British lion crushes the Boers

dug by a burial party with Father O'Leary reading the burial service over Protestant and Catholic alike.

When the search and burial parties had completed their dismal duty, the battalion counted eighteen men killed and sixty-three wounded; since three of the wounded subsequently died, the first Battle of Paardeberg claimed twenty-one lives. Three-quarters of their casualties had occurred during Aldworth's suicidal assault. This was the most costly Canadian military encounter since the war of 1812: the bloodiest Canadian engagement of the South African War. It accounted for more than half of the Royal Canadians' men killed in action and the 123 men wounded during the war, and reducing their effective numbers by 9%. It became known as "Bloody Sunday."

Those who returned to the safety of the main drift were shattered by their first bloody engagement. Haunted by the sounds and sights of the slaughter and the suffering of their comrades, and their sense of failure, some of the men broke down and "wept like children." Others felt hardened by the experience and vowed vengeance.[63] Many simply sat silent and unresponsive, convinced that they "had seen enough of war." Indeed "everyone has had enough," Otter confided to his wife, "if they were honest enough to say so."[64]

A pall of gloom and defeat hung over the Canadians as they awoke on Monday morning, still tired and depressed. The day's obvious failure, tragic loss of life and sense of futility bore heavily on the men and their Commanding Officer. Ever sensitive to public sentiment, Otter attempted to disassociate himself from Aldworth's suicidal assault, though not entirely successfully. Whoever was responsible, the charge was a tragic mistake. "Of all the blunders of this war," one contemporary Canadian commentator wrote, "Paardeberg is perhaps the most unpardonable."[65]

Saner British counsel succeeded Kitchener's mad strategy. The next day Roberts arrived at Paardeberg, recovered from his illness. Alarmed by his army's losses, he vetoed Kitchener's plan to renew the assault, choosing sounder siege tactics. The next eight days the British spent skirmishing, tightening the noose around Cronje's force. The Canadians played their part, taking their turn on outpost duty and on the firing line.

As the days passed, Roberts' siege tactics began to work. Conditions in Cronje's encampment became increasingly parlous. Although they possessed ample ammunition, the physical conditions in the laager, their privations and the apparent hopelessness of their plight began to sap morale. Some of Cronje's officers talked openly about surrender, especially after Cronje refused his able younger lieutenant's advice to escape, stubbornly deciding to stand or fall at Paardeberg.

On 26 February, Kruger, conscious of the seriousness of Cronje's predicament, called for a national prayer vigil. It was the eve of Majuba Day, the nineteenth anniversary of the Boers' spectacular defeat of British troops during the First Boer War of Independence, an event that the Boers celebrated religiously each year. The British military, equally conscious of the date's significance and anxious to avenge their humiliation, decided the time had come to assault the Boer's defences.

The Royal Canadians occupied a prominent place in Roberts' planned night attack on the demoralized Boer entrenchments. Roberts' plans placed Canadians in the lead, since it was their turn to be on the firing line. Assisted by the Gordons, the Shropshires and the Royal Engineers, six Canadian companies were to occupy the most forward British lines. Then at 2:00 a.m., with bayonets fixed and under cover of darkness, they were to rush the Boer trenches about six hundred yards away. Should they encounter difficulties, they were to entrench and wait for assistance.

Warfare in South Africa

True to plan, a few minutes after 2:00 a.m. the Canadians emerged slowly from their trenches, uninterrupted for about forty-five minutes, some of the men holding the sleeve of the man on their left to keep their bearings in the starless darkness. Most men were no more than one hundred yards short of their destination when they encountered the flash and sound of rifle fire, followed by a general fusillade. Boer sentries had detected their approach.

Warned by the premature discharge of the first couple of Boer rifle shots, most of the Canadians threw themselves to the ground just before the fusillade and were spared the full impact of the concentrated Boer fire. The Royal Engineers hastily dug trenches. The thorn scrub, trees and natural gullies close to the river protected H Company from the initial and subsequent Boer rifle fire. The other companies were not so well located. Situated in the open, they bore the brunt of the day's casualties.

As soon as the Canadians dropped to the ground, their front line returned fire while the second line entrenched, and for fifteen minutes a lively battle ensued. Paralyzed by fear, more than one man in the firing line remained glued to his rifle, unable to fire. Sometimes men in the second line substituted their picks and shovels for their rifles and a place in the firing line; some interrupted their digging to aid wounded or dying comrades; others used their shovels as helmets (anticipating Sam Hughes' MacAdam shield-shovel!).

Then, without warning, the Canadians' firing slackened, their line broke and four of the six companies fled back to the security of their trenches. Someone on their left had called out "in an authoritative tone 'retire and bring back your wounded.'" The identity of the person remains unknown. In battle the desire to run is often strong, and those who heard the order or saw the flight remembered the suicidal charge of Bloody Sunday and needed no prompting. As Private F.H. Dunham wryly recalled, "I think all records for the 100 yards were broken that night." Private A. Macaulay in D Company recalled the cries of their wounded and dying, the flashes and sounds of rifle fire, and the darkness, which gave the battle the character of a nightmare.[66] One of his comrades, Private Charles Donaldson, stopped in his flight to carry his mortally wounded corporal, J.M. Thomas, to the safety of the trenches.

Cronje's men

Once the four fleeing companies installed themselves in their trenches, they remained there for the duration of the battle, except for Private Richard Thompson, the medical student from D Company who had saved his friend's life during Bloody Sunday. Just as dawn was breaking, a stretcher-bearer called for a volunteer to bring in a wounded man. Thompson dropped his rifle and ran three hundred yards under fire, arriving just before the wounded man was killed by another bullet. Although both his company captain and Otter recommended him for a Victoria Cross for this and his previous act of heroism, in July 1900 he received instead one of the seven Queen's scarves knitted by Queen Victoria, for distinguished service in the field by private soldiers in designated units. Thompson was the only Canadian to receive a Queen's scarf.

Meanwhile, the two companies closer to the river retained their positions and saved the reputation of their regiment. Alone, they continued to fire for a time to disguise the break in the Canadian lines. Then they waited for dawn, confident that as soon as daylight arrived the Boers would move out of their trenches to investigate; then the Canadians would respond.

As the darkness began to lift and the Boers appeared above their trenches, the Canadians opened fire. An hour or so later the Boer fire slackened, and a white flag appeared. Despite Kruger's prayers, the front-line Boers had had enough. At first, the Canadians misread the signal and continued to fire. Then at about 6:00 a.m., a man carrying a white flag emerged from the trenches and moved toward the Canadian line. Soon groups of Boers began moving out of their trenches, the first party surrendering to the Canadians. Altogether 4,100 persons surrendered. The Canadians had stolen Majuba Day!

Cronje's surrender was a bitter, demoralizing blow. According to General Christiaan De Wet, probably the Boers' cleverest general and subsequently the heart and soul of the resistance, it was "one of the most important chapters in the history of the two republics." Quite apart from their loss of soldiers and *matériel*, Cronje's defeat had a devastating effect on Boer civilian and military leaders; after all, he was the symbol of their historic resistance.[67] Moreover, it opened the road to Bloemfontein and forced the Boers to reconsider their direction of the war.

Much to their initial embarrassment, the Canadians were credited with Cronje's surrender, and soon became "the envy of the army." Shortly after they had buried their dead, Roberts arrived to praise them for their dash and gallantry, words used in his official dispatch to the British government. "Canadian," he asserted, "now stands for bravery, dash and courage." Not to be surpassed, Smith-Dorrien employed his legendary talent for flattery; and even Otter echoed the praise of his superiors. The officers and men of the other battalions were equally complimentary to the Canadians for "wiping out the shame of Majuba."

The exaggerated construction of the Paardeberg victory by the British military authorities and the press was designed to recognize and further encourage colonial military contribu-

Chocolate box and inscribed shell

tions. As the news spread, the Royal Canadians were flooded with wires of congratulations, often couched in extravagant language. The Queen and members of the royal family, the Governor-General, the Prime Minister, the Canadian High Commissioner in London and countless British notables sent their congratulations.

Authorities in Canadian towns and cities, provincial legislatures, commercial, patriotic, educational and voluntary associations joined the chorus of praise. News of the victory and the mention of Canada brought members of the British House of Commons to their feet. Popular British artists such as Canton Woodville and J.P. Beadle hurried to place on canvas a heroic but inaccurate vision of the Canadians' assault on Cronje's laager. At home, news of Paardeberg incited riotous celebrations.

An instant legend had been born. Imperialists acclaimed the victory as the dawn of a new era, a stinging rebuke to Little Englandism. The senior Dominion had avenged Majuba Hill, wiped clean the stain, opened the road to victory and demonstrated to a hostile world the solidity of the Empire. One version of the story claimed that "few of this gallant Company of Great Britain's defenders could speak English."[68] To nationalists, Paardeberg had been a victory of their citizen soldiers, "who charged like veterans," a bold assertion of nationhood, a declaration "to the world that a new power had arisen in the west." Both imperialists and nationalists were convinced that Paardeberg would be the basis of a new patriotism.[69]

Contemporaries told and retold the Paardeberg story.

They recounted how the "mostly beardless youths" had "jumped like race horses, and had "made a charge which will live in history." The men themselves realized that the victory "was not quite as satisfactory and complete as we hoped for, and that it had as much to do with chance as to courage,"[70] but soon they too began to repeat the rhetoric of how the smartest Boer general had surrendered to them. According to one version, the knowledge that the Canadians were in the trenches filled the Boers with fear and forced their surrender. They recounted how Boer prisoners had remarked, "You are not men you are devils. We can stand the shooting of the average British soldier but your Canadians are regular fire-eaters.…It's easy to see now what nation is going to rule the world."[71]

The Battle of Paardeberg, which includes both Bloody Sunday and the surrender of Cronje's laager, became an instant symbol of Canadian military prowess. For fifty years and more, Canada's Boer War veterans from all units met annually in ever-decreasing numbers to remember and celebrate Paardeberg Day, an anniversary observed still by the Royal Canadian Regiment of Infantry. Imperialists attempted to export Paardeberg and make it an imperial commemoration; and for a brief time it was celebrated in Australia.[72] In the early years, veterans organized elaborate demonstrations, culminating in a banquet, whose menus featured delicacies such as Canadian Emergency Rations with Muddy Spruit Sauce, Clear De Wet Soup, Roast Beef a la Trek Oxen and Gravy à la Cronje. While the humour soon died, the Paardeberg myth has enjoyed a hardy life.

The myth focuses little attention on Bloody Sunday's tragic failure or the flight of the four companies during the battle at Cronje's laager. Nor does it appreciate the extent to which Cronje's surrender was the result of siege rather than assault.[73] The Royal Canadians, however, had good reason for pride. During the grim ten-day battle, this contingent of citizen soldiers had displayed courage, stamina and tenacity. They had proven themselves equal to the much-vaunted British Regulars. The steadiness of the two companies was more than accident or chance. In short, the Canadians had played an important role in securing one of Britain's greatest victories of the war.

8

THE MONTREAL FLAG RIOT

Conflict at home mitigated Paardeberg's 'nation-building' potential.[74] Although Canada's decision to send troops to South Africa had dampened, it had not dissipated the animosities of the fanatical few. There were still those determined to turn the war into an ethnic contest, pitching French Canadian against English Canadian. Nowhere were these ethno-linguistic tensions more acute than in the bi-ethnic city of Montreal, where Hugh Graham's Montreal *Star* had led a hysterical, politically partisan and dangerous campaign to enlist Canadian participation in the war. By the late 1890s, Montreal consisted of a geographic patchwork of fairly self-contained communities defined by language, class and creed, and held together by a fragile mutual respect for each group's linguistic, social and religious space. The Montreal riot challenged that peace, revealed the misunderstanding and mistrust behind the city's placid contemporary facade and served as a wake-up call to sensitive political leaders.

Initially, most Canadians greeted news of their troops' role in Britain's first major victory since Black Week with bells, music, flags, bunting and noisy street parades. Municipal offices closed; students left classes and many employees joined

Medical students march

the exuberant and often inebriated demonstrations. Paardeberg together with two other British victories, the liberation of Kimberley and the relief of Ladysmith, triggered 'victory' celebrations throughout the Empire that were more appropriate to the war's end.

In Montreal, bells, flags and bunting announced the Paardeberg victory on the morning of 1 March. In contrast to the punishing South African heat faced by Canada's recently minted heroes, Montrealers were digging out from the season's worst snowstorm, in temperatures that one journal described as the coldest since 1869. McGill University's students, led by raucous medical students, quit their 9:00 a.m. classes to celebrate their country's victories. Waving stolen and borrowed flags and bunting, and singing patriotic songs, about five hundred students trooped their boisterous way along University Street. They invaded the adjacent Montreal High School, liberated its students from their morning prayers, and together they marched to Dominion Square where the Montreal *Star* had erected a large news bulletin. There they lighted a bonfire and continued their noisy demonstration, singing, chanting, and waving flags and banners; and cheering the *Star's* latest bulletins from the front, announcing the heroic deaths and

McGill University

suspect than the editors of franchophone journals who had opposed Canadian participation in the war. When the mob reached Place d'Armes, no flag was flying from the masthead of *La Patrie*. It did not help that the journal's editors were the sons of Israel Tarte, the man most imperialists held responsible for the government's initial reticence and opposition to the dispatch of troops. The crowd immediately ordered *La Patrie* to hoist the Union Jack. The journal complied, though reluctantly, opposed more to the method than the request. But when one student attempted to remove a Paul Kruger button from a journalist's coat, a fight ensued and windows were broken.

injuries of Canadian young men, affirming and validating the borders of imperial rule — conscious that there were several McGill students among their numbers.

The students were soon joined by a growing body of townsmen and fortified by free beer distributed by Hugh Graham's *Star*. After an hour or more of liquid celebration a mob, now estimated at some two thousand, inspired by the deeds of their soldier compatriots in South Africa, decided to establish the imperial character of their own city. Their destinations were the bastions of "suspected disloyalty," the offices of several francophone journals close to City Hall. Armed with signs, stolen flags and bunting, they marched toward the commercial sector of the old city, singing songs and chanting slogans, including "Soldiers of the Queen," "Rule Britannia," the "Maple Leaf Forever" and an endless rendition of "God Save the Queen." Some of their choral improvisations were more tailored to their mission and the season:

> *There is a place where they don't shovel snow.*
> *That is the place that the Boers ought to go.*

The crowd possessed no doubt as to the identity of the local Boers. They were French Canadians. None were more

The "Main," Montreal

Place d'Armes

The crowd then moved off to secure another perceived enemy outpost, *La Presse*, a moderate, independent journal that had supported Canadian participation from the beginning — a subtlety lost on the indiscriminate crowd. Vastly outnumbered, the small *La Presse* staff soon succumbed and hoisted a small Union Jack. *Le Journal*, a pro-war Conservative newspaper, received a similar visit and the mob secured a comparable victory. Then it moved on to City Hall, where the City Mayor, Raymond Préfontaine, the Liberal Member of Parliament for Maisonneuve and an outspoken imperialist, welcomed the crowd, called for imperial solidarity and granted all his civic employees a half-holiday.

The appeased mob then began to disperse, all except a hard core of McGill University students intent on additional mischief.[75] They decided to return home by way of the Université Laval de Montréal, located at the corner of St. Denis and Ste. Catherine streets. It was shortly after noon when the McGill crowd reached Laval, a time when most of the students were at dinner. The McGill mob had no difficulty, therefore, persuading the lonely caretaker to raise a Union Jack.

But when the Laval students returned from their lunch and learned of the noon visitation, they cut the Union Jack from its pole and organized a counter-demonstration to regain control of their city and assert a contrary view of the war. All afternoon some nine hundred people, Laval students and their supporters, roamed the streets carrying the tricolour, the Red Ensign, the Canadian flag as *Les Débats* described it — and one Union Jack, and singing "La Marseillaise" and other French songs. Along the way they demanded that all French language newspapers replace the Union Jacks with tricolours, and physically removed the Union Jack from the *La Presse* building. The Union Jack on the Montreal *Star* was also removed. "They cheered the Queen's statue in Victoria

[From La Patrie.]

French-Canadian counter-demonstration

Square," the student weekly *McGill Outlook*, piously reported, "but on one occasion at least, men in their procession were heard to utter very uncomplimentary remarks — not to mention a stronger adjective — about Her Gracious Majesty — as well as their enemies at McGill."[76] While no great physical damage had been done during the morning demonstration or the afternoon counter-demonstration, both had kindled a spark.

In the evening a mixed crowd of McGill students, townsmen and ruffians, armed with frozen potatoes, sticks, iron bars, and according to one report, guns assembled in front of Laval. The Laval University authorities had anticipated violence, and had requested police protection. Six patrol wagons arrived with instructions to preserve order without arresting anyone, if possible. After a brief scuffle over a flag that the McGill students had planted in a snowbank, the police decided to disperse the crowd in order to avoid an escalation of violence. They shut off all the lights in the Laval building and turned six cold-water hoses on the crowd. Those who were showered were immediately encased in ice, as it was still bitterly cold. After a brief and unsuccessful struggle with the men handling the hose, the angry mob responded by breaking "every window" in the building. Scuffles ensued, and the Laval students, backed by the city's police,[77] reinforced by some townsmen from Coteau St. Louis, drove the McGill students and their supporters back to their quarter.

News of the previous night's events spread rapidly, creating fear and apprehension in the city and abroad. The Montreal *Herald*, profoundly embarrassed by the previous day's events, disassociated the English community from the riot, condemned the McGill students, and singled out the *Star* and its editor for a severe reprimand. In its opinion those who used the flag to cloak their partisan interests — were traitors to Canada and the Empire. Similarly, McGill's Dean of Law wrote his distinguished counterpart at the Université Laval, apologizing for the unfortunate incident.

In Ottawa the Prime Minister, a former McGill student himself, informed the Governor-General of his fears and wired Mayor Préfontaine, asking him to intervene to establish and maintain order. The Prime Minister also wrote to his friend the Archbishop of Montreal, Monseigneur Paul Bruchesi, who served as Vice-Rector of Laval, asking him to intervene and if necessary to apologize for the Laval students' alleged destruction of a Union Jack. Israel Tarte was not amused by his leader's intervention and begged the Archbishop to do nothing of the sort, since the English respected only those who stood up to them, who looked them in the eye,[78] advice that Tarte repeated in the columns of *La Patrie*.[79]

The Governor-General was equally alarmed, and wired the British government of this serious turn of events.[80] His intelligence was not reassuring. "No lives have been lost so far," Minto informed the British Colonial Secretary. "But there is cause for anxiety and the feeling between French and English runs very high."[81] The Director of Dominion Police, A. P. Sherwood, had just returned from Montreal and warned him to expect more trouble and predicted that the Militia may have to be called out. Minto, who also served as McGill University's Visitor, wrote to its Principal, William Peterson, asking for a report and begging that "nothing be done to accentuate present difficulties,"[82] insisting that "the lot of the two races in Canada had been thrown together and it should be the duty of us all to enlist the dual machinery that must exist to run smoothly as it can."[83]

Laurier's and Minto's apprehension grew more acute as tensions spread to other Canadian campuses. The students from Queen's and the University of Toronto offered to assist their McGill comrades;[84] and Université Laval's Quebec City campus, where a small scuffle had broken out between its students and some English the previous day in front of *L'Evènement*, made a comparable offer. Meanwhile, Préfontaine, under pressure from various quarters, wrote to McGill's Principal and the Archbishop and Vice-Rector of Laval, asking them to call a truce to help prevent further disorder.[85] Then he arranged a meeting between the Principal and the Archbishop, at which Peterson protested that McGill students were not solely responsible for the damage to Laval's building and apologized for the behaviour of his students. Peterson, who spoke French fluently, repeated his apology before the Laval students, promised to pay damages, and asked that all plans for further demonstrations cease. The Archbishop repeated Peterson's call for peace. The President of Laval's medical students made a conciliatory speech, professing Laval's loyalty,[86] and the students responded graciously with three cheers for McGill and its Principal. All seemed to point to an end of the tensions.

But peace had not returned to Montreal. The Director of Dominion Police was right: there would be more violence as the torch of revenge passed to the larger citizenry, who were unaware of or indifferent to the truce. Determined to regain control of their city and avenge the injury, an angry crowd, estimated at several thousand, assembled in Victoria Square that evening bearing French flags, singing French songs and ripping British flags from adjacent buildings — one of which was trampled underfoot. After an hour or so the appeased

Lord Minto

crowd began to disperse, leaving behind a militant remnant to bear the brunt of a growing and ugly English mob. A free-for-all broke out. The police appeared but failed to control the crowd and, fearing the arrival of the Orange contingent from Griffintown, they advised the Mayor to call out the Militia. The Mayor was prepared for this request, conscious of the potential seriousness of the situation and the weakness of the city's police force.

The morning of 3 March broke on a tense city under Militia surveillance. Canadian troops in Montreal protected French and English Canadians from each other while their comrades of both languages were fighting and dying together in South Africa; this tragic spectacle was not lost on the Canadian people. The demonstrations, however, had ended and peace seemed to have been restored. The physical damage that had been caused by the two days of sporadic rioting was not extensive.

More lasting and damaging, however, was the legacy of ill feelings, distrust and misunderstanding engendered by the riot, and which was not so easily dissipated. The riot would become a bitter historic reference, another example of English Canadian disregard for French Canadian linguistic and religious rights.

While the Militia patrolled peaceful streets, Montreal's newspapers locked in a fierce battle of words. Indeed, the verbal battle had begun before the last physical blows had been struck. The Montreal *Star*, assailed on all sides, defended itself and the McGill students. It railed against its accusers, dismissed the affair as a "boyish frolic" that had resulted in some hurt feelings and a broken pane of glass. In its view it had been merely a student prank, a patriotic parade that simply got out of hand;[87] an explanation that deserves some greater credence than its self-interested source might suggest.

While university demonstrations and pranks were fairly common at the time, clearly the McGill demonstration had gone beyond the bounds of propriety and touched a sensitive civic nerve. The English mob's march, their symbolic control of the streets, had an unmistakably provocative and menacing political message. Their indiscriminate attack on the French language dailies, oblivious to the various journals' subtle differences and changing attitudes on the war, demonstrated a depth of

Montrealers debate the war

of hounds, thirsty for blood and intent on insulting the flag and symbols of their nationality. In its opinion, if the McGill students, the future leaders of English Canada, behaved in this outrageous manner, the future for this country was bleak indeed. The editors of *Les Débats* agreed with *La Patrie*. French Canadians must now prepare for the worst: if the Boers had three hundred thousand

dangerous misunderstanding "not only amongst the ignorant masses but men of education from whom our world would expect more sober behaviour."[88]

The students, however, had acted within a social environment that had been poisoned by the verbal abuse and violence of the yellow press. Consequently French Canadians construed the students' actions as giving substance to the more extreme English opinions within the country. *La Presse* labelled the incident "La Guerre à Montreal," and noted sarcastically that McGill students preferred to fight in Canada than to defend the British flag in Africa.[89] *La Patrie* agreed: forcing a French Canadian to raise a flag when he was outnumbered a hundred to one was no way to instill loyalty. In its editors' view, the riot was but one of a series of violent assaults on French Canada, dating back to the Rebellion Losses Bill of 1849.

La Patrie believed that little more was needed to destroy the federal pact. French Canadians must now prepare themselves for the worst, even the end of Confederation. Meanwhile, French Canadians must defend themselves and their property with all the means at their disposal.[90] *Les Débats*, a strident nationalist, pro-Boer paper, was more alarmist still. It spoke ominously of civil war, a 'race' war provoked by a crude pack

people, French Canadians had three million, plus the help of their Franco-American cousins and the undoubted assistance of France.[91]

Canada's leaders were shaken by the Montreal riot and the subsequent war of words. Frightened by what they had seen, they moved at once to restore harmony and moderation. In the House of Commons, the riot provoked a lively debate. When Alexander McNeil, the Irish-born Conservative Member of Parliament for Bruce North, blamed the trouble in Montreal on Tarte and *La Patrie*, working in tandem with Boer secret agents, he was rebuked by George Eulas Foster, a prominent member of his own party. Tarte himself did nothing to calm tempers. Still furious, he refused to be reconciled. Had he been in the offices of *La Patrie*, he informed the House, he would have died rather than hoist the British flag. Even John Charlton attempted to broker a peace, condemning the McGill students and exonerating the Laval students.[92]

The threats, excuses and insults, however, were soon submerged by more moderate voices, ready to identify and rebuke the offenders, the "overbearing" and impudent McGill students,[93] and call for respect, understanding and a restoration of peaceful coexistence. The Toronto *Globe*, probably prompted by political considerations, led the way in a long

French Canadian soldiers

lecture addressed to English Canadian extremists, more especially those in the Tory party:

> A loyalty that is the product of terrorism
> is a poor thing. An Imperialism that must be
> forced by clamour and riot would be a curse
> rather than a blessing to Canada. There must
> be freedom here for the French-speaking
> citizen as well as for the English-speaking
> citizen. To cut this country in two by a line
> of racial cleavage would be an unspeakable
> evil to Canada and a betrayal of the best
> traditions of the British Empire. [94]

Other Liberal Ontario dailies followed the *Globe's* lead, attempting to dissolve the ethno-linguistic dispute into a partisan quarrel, blaming the whole thing on their political opponents' intolerance. The Tory journals rose to the bait, blaming the Liberals for the ethno-linguistic misunderstandings.[95] The Toronto *World* took an even harder line, refusing to reform or repent. The Montreal riot, it bluntly contended, was but another instance of separatist strength in Quebec that remained unchecked owing to its political utility.

In Britain the Montreal Flag Riot received extensive coverage, perhaps because it challenged the myth of a liberal empire, and its vaunted unity in diversity, of which Canada was the reigning example. Some British journals dismissed the incident as trivial, though they feared more serious consequences if English Canadian zeal remained unchecked. The *St. James' Gazette*, for example, warned its readers not to attach too much attention to the events in Montreal, comparing the riot to a similar battle between Cambridge students and the police, provoked by news of the relief of Ladysmith.[96] It noted the difference between the two events, however, more particularly the dangerous linguistic lines that divided the rioters in Montreal, and warned Montrealers that patriotism cannot be forced on a reluctant people.[97] Most regretted the incident and pleaded for better relations between the two peoples in the interests of imperial harmony and national unity.

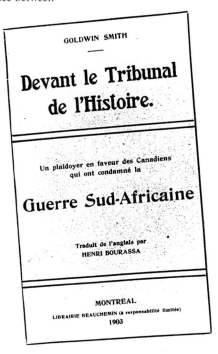

GOLDWIN SMITH

Devant le Tribunal de l'Histoire.

Un plaidoyer en faveur des Canadiens qui ont condamné la

Guerre Sud-Africaine

Traduit de l'anglais par
HENRI BOURASSA

MONTREAL
LIBRAIRIE BEAUCHEMIN (à responsabilité limitée)
1903

Bourassa's anti-war sentiments echoed many French-Canadian concerns

Even in Montreal the war of words soon ceased. Embarrassed by their crude physical and verbal confrontation, French and English Canadians soon retreated behind their silent but deceptive facades, muttering words of reconciliation and goodwill. *La Presse* led the way. In the name of all French Canadians, it reaffirmed its loyalty to Britain and its support for the war. The *Mail and Empire* responded generously by regretting the indiscriminate attack on *La Presse*, "an able and responsible journal...that has from the start uttered loyal and indeed cordial sentiments toward Britain in this struggle." Even *La Patrie's* anger soon cooled. While it had supported the Laval counter-demonstration, insisting that the protesters had carried a Union Jack and acclaimed the Queen at Victoria Square,[98] it apologized for the conduct of French Canadian hotheads. The youth on both sides, it wrote in a moment of goodwill and tolerance, ought to be excused for, "Qui de nous n'a pas eu vingt ans."[99] *La Patrie* seemed strangely to have accepted the Montreal *Star's* interpretation that the riot had been little more than a student prank that got out of hand.

La Patrie's dismissive summation of the riot, however, was less perceptive and convincing. Despite the profession of goodwill, feelings remained tender. Nine days after the riot, Laval students at first refused McGill's invitation to join McGill and Bishops College students in the elaborate Montreal demonstration marking the departure of Lord Strathcona's Horse, a battal-

Lucien Larue, French Canadian soldier killed in South Africa

ion of scouts raised by McGill's wealthy Chancellor, Lord Strathcona.[100] Moreover, the Montreal riot was a stern warning to pragmatic Canadian politicians toying with notions of imperial reorganization. It suggested the limits and dangers of imperialism in a bi-national country. "The day is coming," Laurier informed his compatriots, "when this country will have to take its place among the nations of the earth... I do not want my country's independence to be reached through the blood of civil war."

Scarcely a month after the riot, during a pre-election tour of Quebec, Sir Charles Tupper, the canny old Conservative leader, attempted to distance himself from imperialism, boasting that he had smashed the old Imperial Federation League and denouncing Laurier for being too imperialist for him. Even the Governor-General, an erstwhile imperialist, began to understand the complexities of Canadian governance and the limits of imperialism in Canada. Convinced that the "racial hatred" generated by the war had "been positively wicked" and the "conversation of English society here repeated to me foolish in the extreme,"[101] Minto made concerted efforts to bridge the gap between the country's elites.

The Montreal riot served as a wake-up call to the country's leaders, sensitizing them to the implications of imperialism in a bi-national country. Regrettably, however, it remained a reference point of distrust and apprehension for many years to come.[102]

Departure of Strathcona's Horse from Montreal days after the riot.

9

THE FRACTURED RETURN

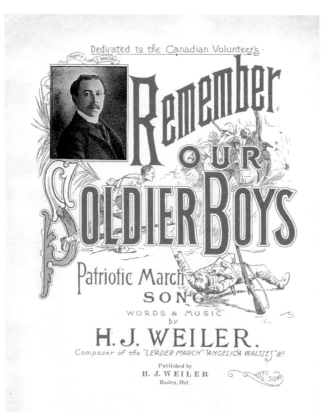

Paardeberg had forged a temporary *esprit de corps* among the Royal Canadians. It had also altered the nature of warfare. After Paardeberg foot soldiers were relegated increasingly to guard, police and outpost duty, secondary service in support of the more mobile mounted troops. Vulnerable to division and assigned to sedentary postings, the Canadians' battle-bred fraternity quickly fragmented, as so painfully demonstrated by their divisive conflict with Otter over their return to Canada.

Although the British hoped to repeat their Paardeberg success, Cronje's capture and the death of the Boers' Commander-in-Chief, Piet Joubert, a month later changed Boer leadership and strategy. A new generation of leaders, Christiaan De Wet, Jacobus de la Rey, Louis Botha and Jan Smuts assumed control, determined to have no more Paardebergs, no more great pitched battles with high stakes.

Instead they would employ more unconventional tactics.

They would attack the British lines of transportation and communication, and through ambush, harassment and hit-and-run tactics, make British occupation untenable. They would pursue the war to its bitter end, targeting Roberts' large, cumbersome force, so dependent upon extended supply lines. As for the British, they would continue their more conventional warfare until they occupied the capitals of the two Boer republics. Then they would annex the territory and retaliate with a dirtier war of farm burning and concentration camps, operating outside the conventional rules of warfare.

During the inclement weeks following Paardeberg, the Canadians' morale declined precipitously as the newly proclaimed heroes made their slow, ragged progress toward Bloemfontein, spectators of the skirmishes retarding their occupation of the Orange Free State capital. Upon entering Bloemfontein on 15 March, the men discovered that there were worse things than fighting.

Christiaan De Wet's sash

Their camp, initially "a green grassy plain" a quarter of a mile outside the city, soon became an unhealthy muddy swamp; it became their home for over a month, while the British Army refurbished and planned its great march to Pretoria.

Without tents, the men constructed two-person shacks by dropping a blanket over a lanyard tied to a rifle barrel, the butt of the rifle planted firmly in the ground. Their ground-sheets served as a floor; and at night they shared their blankets and greatcoats. Much of their clothing was missing, worn or patched. Shirts had no buttons, trousers had no knees or seats, and boots had no soles. Men fashioned trousers from sacking or made one shirt out of two. They were so poorly clad that when they went to Bloemfontein for provisions, they combined clothing from several comrades to appear decently dressed.

Crude shanties used by soldiers

Illness, the plague of all sedentary camps, devastated the Bloemfontein camp. An epidemic of enteric fever sapped the contingent's strength, eroded morale, and played havoc with its organization and administration. Three weeks after the battalion reached Bloemfontein, its effective strength had been reduced from 740 to 550. "Things are getting serious here," Private Albert Perkins confided to his diary on 23 March. "Men are getting sick continually….There are many others who cannot stick it out very much longer."

Bloemfontein's atrocious medical services were infinitely worse than at Belmont. A chronic shortage of medical accommodation, personnel, supplies and occasionally food made a bad situation desperate. As the New Brunswick schoolteacher in G Company, Russell Hubly, wrote: "I have seen men in high fever, lying on nothing but a blanket between them and the ground and too weak…to pick the vermin from their clothes. In the same tent were men so weak from dysentery, that in the absence of an orderly, their clothing became filthy."[103] An exposé written by the American journalist, William Burdett-Coutts, created a public outcry in Britain and led to the appointment of a Royal Commission of Inquiry that dismissed the medical deficiencies in Bloemfontein as one of the cruel necessities of warfare.

Morale plummeted as sickness increased and camp conditions deteriorated. The men's disillusionment and dissatisfaction revived the unit's national, regional and personal tensions and focused on the Commanding Officer. Men won-

Boer prisoners

dered if Otter had any idea of their living conditions, the state of their campground, the lice and the dirt, the absence of tents, their lack of new clothing and want of recreational facilities. They asked themselves why a Canadian battalion waited longer than a British unit for its provisions. They noted that neighbouring British battalions received sporting equipment and musical instruments. They wondered if things would be different under another Commanding Officer.

The arrival of a backlog of mail from home brought Otter even more grief. Many of the old Belmont grievances, embroidered in letters to friends and family back home, had been published in the press. Otter was blamed unfairly for failing to report sufficiently frequently on his contingent, notably for the delay and initial inaccuracy of the casualty list from Bloody Sunday, as well as his 'misappropriation' of regimental funds to purchase comforts for the men's Christmas dinner.

Furious, and fearful that the criticism would do nothing to advance his career, Otter paraded his battalion in the pouring rain and berated them for half an hour, informing them that one of them was a "Goddamn liar."[104] Stung by the Christmas dinner charges, Otter ordered the Captain of C Company to write a rejoinder to the press contradicting the anonymous letter in the Toronto papers.

The men were not impressed. "All the boys in camp think that the letters read by the Colonel were just right," Private Albert Perkins wrote in his diary on 25 March, "and I do,

too." "I don't think any of the fellows, not many at least, out here would volunteer to come out again if they were to get a Victoria Cross," another man wrote to his friend back home to dissuade him from joining the Royal Canadians' [one-hundred-man] draft being conducted to replace the unit's casualties.[105] This was no way to run a battalion.

By May, Roberts was ready for his 290-mile, five-week march to Pretoria. The British divided their overwhelming force into two columns, one under the command of General Ian Hamilton and the other under Roberts' direct command, one on either side of the rail. The Canadians, numbering no more than 611 in all, were assigned to Hamilton's column. The road to Pretoria was far from an open highway. The Boers impeded their progress wherever possible, disrupting the rail and telegraph lines and challenging them at strategic locations.

Along the way, the Canadians fought battles at Israel's Poort, Thaba 'Nchu, Zand River and Doornkop. The first two were clearing operations fought before the march began. In all the battles the battalion acquitted itself with honour and incurred casualties. At Israel's Poort one man was killed and three were wounded including Otter, who receive a slight wound on his chin and neck. He was taken from the field in a stretcher to a field hospital, then on to Bloemfontein where he procured private quarters rather than trust himself to a military hospital. Although fit to rejoin his battalion within two weeks, lack of transport prevented his return for a month. During Otter's absence, his jovial second-in-

Boer commandos

command, Lawrence Buchan, took command. His leadership style was appreciated by his battalion and by senior British officers alike.

Otter returned to the battalion just in time to lead his diminutive force of 443 men across the Vaal, the first infantry battalion to enter the Transvaal. The Royal Canadians fought their last battle at Doornkop before reaching Pretoria. Although some historians describe the battle as little more than an heroic but costly charge to redeem Hamilton's reputation, contemporaries represented it as clearing the road to Johannesburg, thereby crippling the Boers' access to gold to purchase *matériel* abroad. On 5 June Roberts entered Pretoria.

Boers in camp

At this point, the British higher command was convinced that the war was at an end, except for mopping up. By the end of September, they had seized the Boers' railways, occupied their capitals, had dispersed "the last compact and centrally organized Boer force" at Belfast and had won a major battle at Bradwater Basin. President Kruger had fled to Europe and the population of the Transvaal and the Orange Free State appeared demoralized and ready to come to terms. On 25 October 1900, the British formally annexed the two republics. Thereafter those who continued to resist British authority were considered rebels, bereft of rights and privileges. Robert himself prepared to leave and turn over command to Kitchener.

Although the conventional war had ended, it was soon replaced by a more mobile, dirty war of guerrilla tactics, concentration camps and farm burning — a conflict that would last for almost another two years. The British found it increasingly difficult to hold what they had conquered and to provide law and order, transportation and communication, and the semblance of a civil society. To purchase greater security, they assigned a quarter of their troops to defend their lines of communication.

Meanwhile Boer soldiers one day were peaceful farmers the next. Their farms were a source of refuge, intelligence and supply, managed effectively by women. Both those who favoured the cause and those who doubted it (the so-called 'hands-uppers') were hostage to the guerrilla's demands. To eliminate this tactical advantage, the British instituted a scorched earth policy and began burning the farms of men still on commando, driving their women, children and servants out onto the veldt, forcing their men to feed and protect them. The enormity of this policy obliged the British to adopt a more 'permanent' solution: the concentration camp, a place to protect, feed and care for the women, children, old men and Black servants of the Boer soldiers on commando, as well as the 'hands-uppers.'

Altogether some sixty-eight camps were established, segregated by race, gender and loyalty. While there were a few 'model' camps, most were places of death, disease and malnutrition, the most common diseases being measles, pneumonia and dysentery; conditions in the Black camps were even more primitive, as they were deprived of medical assistance. During the course of the war, as many as twenty-eight thousand Boer women, children and old men died in the concentration camps. Out of some sixty thousand, the number of deaths represented a quarter of the women and children in the two Boer republics; another estimated sixteen thousand Blacks met a similar fate, a condition exposed by the courageous British crusader Emily Hobhouse.[106] Little wonder the Boer women's bitter memories fuelled the subsequent Afrikaner nationalist movement for generations.[107]

The second part of Roberts' and his successor Kitchener's strategy to subdue the recalcitrant Boers was their scorched earth policy, the systematic destruction of Boer farms and crops, designed to starve the diehards into submission. The two former republics were divided into sections defined by barbed wire connected to blockhouses within shooting range of one another, manned by three or four soldiers. Within these perimeters, long columns of soldiers scoured the land, destroying every crop or building and rounding up all inhabitants.

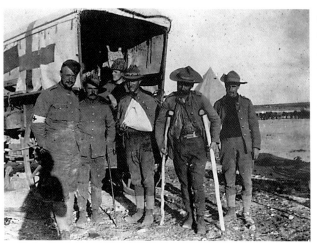

While this new war placed a premium on mounted men, the army still needed infantry for sedentary deployment, to retain their gains and protect

Medics tend to weary troops

the army's supply lines; consequently the imperial authorities pressed colonial troops to extend their service. Soon after the Canadians reached Pretoria, they were consigned to line-of-communication duty and asked to guard rails, telegraph, water and supply lines, and the occasional prisoner, a routine broken for only ten days in August when they participated in an attempt to capture Christiaan De Wet—foot soldiers chasing mounted men! More detrimental to regimental unity was the decision to divide the Royal Canadians and consign them to five separate stations. Comfortably housed, healthy and well-fed, the battalion's strength climbed to 663, as men returned from hospitals. But separation did little for regimental solidarity.

Most of the Royal Canadians, however, were in no mood to extend their service. Many were tired and disillusioned with war. Others worried about their neglected civilian employment. They had expected to serve for only six months; they had no desire to extend their one-year contract, and they considered their claim to return at least as valid as that of London's City Imperial Volunteers.

Otter, aware of the approaching termination of his battalion's service contract, had approached his superiors for instruction but received no response. Finally he communicated directly with Roberts' military secretary. Two weeks later, Roberts replied, asking Otter to consider extending his battalion's service until the end of the war. Confident that the war's

end was close, and conscious of the restlessness of the Australians and other colonial troops, Roberts had hoped the Canadians would serve as an example. After consulting only a few officers on his station, Otter agreed immediately, and published his decision in a regimental order.

The six companies at the three other stations were furious. Earlier in the day they had received a contradictory message. Colonel Barker, the officer commanding the lines of communication, had requested the names of all those who would voluntarily extend their service. The men interpreted Barker's request as a communication from the Canadian government. The cancellation of Barker's order fed their suspicion that Otter had attempted to pre-empt their choice. The more they talked, the more recalcitrant they became. In January, Private Albert Perkins had predicted that Otter would get roasted some day. The time had come to turn up the heat!

The officers at the other stations informed Otter, in strongly worded language, that their men refused to extend their service and that they resented his failure to consult them. Otter wrote immediately to Roberts, explaining that he had misjudged the men and that "the large majority" of his officers and men cannot "with justice to themselves or families re-engage."[108] Undeterred by Otter's response, Roberts attempted to reverse the decision. He asked Otter to re-canvass the men, reassuring them that the war would end soon, and that he hoped for their participation in the annexation ceremonies scheduled shortly in Pretoria. He also suggested that the Queen herself would "honour with her presence" those who complied with his request. Otter relayed Roberts' message to all the stations, asking them to reply as soon as possible.

Neither Otter nor Roberts had long to wait. Within two days all the stations had reported. The result was worse than Otter had expected. Deeply embarrassed by the turn of events, Otter apologetically informed Roberts that only three

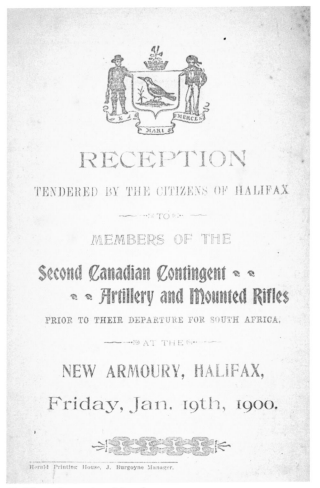

RECEPTION

TENDERED BY THE CITIZENS OF HALIFAX

TO

MEMBERS OF THE

Second Canadian Contingent

Artillery and Mounted Rifles

PRIOR TO THEIR DEPARTURE FOR SOUTH AFRICA,

AT THE

NEW ARMOURY, HALIFAX,

Friday, Jan. 19th, 1900.

Herald Printing House, J. Burgoyne Manager.

Halifax welcomes its soldiers home

hundred men would remain. The rest wanted an immediate passage to Canada.

Otter correctly interpreted the response as a want of confidence in his command. He was wrong, however, to blame his officers for their lack of patriotism and sense of duty, especially his popular second-in-command, Major Lawrence Buchan, who he was convinced had fermented the discontent, despite the fact that Buchan chose to remain.

Although Otter assured Roberts that three hundred men would stay, in fact only 262 did so, whereas 462 left (61%). The majority of those who remained had no choice: they were men from the permanent militia and reinforcements whose time had not expired. Few who remained were happy with their decision. They blamed Otter for their misfortune and his handling of the entire affair.

As soon as Roberts received Otter's second report, he ordered his staff to arrange for the dissenting Canadians' immediate return. Eight days later, on 24 September, the returning men, under the command of Pelletier, left their stations for Pretoria, where Roberts graciously inspected them and thanked them for their service. Then they boarded a train for Cape Town, a two-day journey in cramped, open boxcars, where they boarded the SS *Idaho* for Halifax.

In Halifax they were all heroes. The city had planned a grand reception. A thirty-five-gun salute greeted the ship as it approached the dock. A guard of honour supplied by the recently recruited 3rd Battalion of the Royal Canadian Regiment of Infantry (raised to relieve the British garrison in Halifax for service in South Africa) formed an honour guard; and a band played "The Maple Leaf Forever." A thanksgiving service followed. Then they marched to the armoury through noisy crowded streets decorated with flags, banners and welcoming signs, where the city had prepared an elaborate banquet. While the men feasted, groups of schoolchildren sang patriotic songs and dignitaries showered the men with

London's reception

Royal Canadians' London reception

praise and commendation.

Hometowns feted their return, newspapers hailed their arrival; poets sang their praises:

Canadian heroes hailing home,
War-torn and tempest smitten,
Who circled leagues of rolling foam,
To hold the earth for Britain.[109]

Meanwhile back in South Africa, things deteriorated. Those left behind envied their departing comrades. "It's like the last link with home broken," one man recorded in his diary. Many regretted their decision to remain and sought every opportunity to reverse it. When Kitchener attempted to negotiate the terms of their extended service, the men adamantly refused his proposal that the new terms read 'until the end of war': they would not even consider a three-month

extension. Two or three weeks were all they would countenance, and in this they were backed by the Australian troops. Otter's attempt to negotiate a compromise with Kitchener's office failed, whereupon Otter gave his men two days to make up their minds. In twenty-four hours he had his response: not one man would remain. Once again he had to report his failure to his superiors.

The folly of retaining the men became more obvious daily. Morale plummeted and men became quarrelsome. Drinking, theft and insubordination increased, and although Otter punished, paraded and lectured the men, nothing seemed to work. The whole situation had gotten quite out of hand. Finally, six days after the annexation ceremonies in Cape Town, the Canadians were ordered to leave in three consignments, the first that evening and the other two the next day.

Smith-Dorrien visited their camp, thanked them for their service and received an appreciative reception. Then, packed into "beastly" low open cattle cars whose "floors were covered with manure," the 'Paardeberg heroes' made their slow, seven-day journey to Cape Town, the trains moving only during the day, and the first three days in cold, heavy rains. Cramped, cold and often hungry, many men questioned imperial gratitude. Canadian civilians resented the treatment afforded "the heroes of Paardeberg," particularly when British volunteers left for the Cape "three days later in saloon carriages."[110]

All this changed in Cape Town. Within hours of reaching Cape Town, the Royal Canadians boarded the comfortable, well-stocked *Hawarden Castle* for a pleasant, twenty-two day cruise to Southampton. Generally free from the drudgery of military duties, the men created few difficulties. Although many would have preferred to go home directly, the British authorities seemed set upon sending them home via England, still hoping to encourage colonial recruitment.

At Southampton, a Colonial Troops Entertainment Committee, chaired by the Duke of Abercorn met the vessel. It had arranged thirteen days of elaborate entertainment, lavishly reported and illustrated in the British journals. It began at Southampton with music and speeches. Then the men boarded a train for London where they were met at Addison Station by the Duke and his committee and escorted by the Royal Horse Guard, the Scots Guards' band and the Coldstream Guards' fife and drum band through streets packed with cheering spectators to Kensington Barracks.

The next day they were escorted to and from Windsor Castle, through cheering crowds, to see Queen Victoria for one of her last official acts before her death in January 1901. After the royal salute, the Queen sent for Otter to thank him and to inquire about the sick and wounded. The battalion then marched past the Queen in sections of four, to the tune of "Vive la Canadienne," after which Canada's 'soldiers of the Queen' reformed in a quarter-column in front of her. In a "strong, clear voice," she welcomed and thanked the men, regretted the high casualties, and wished them a safe return, to which Otter responded graciously.

The overwhelming entertainment schedule included a city sightseeing tour the next day that preceded the Lord Mayor's Guildhall reception. The following day they were the guests of a church service in Westminster Abbey, and so it went: tours of Buckingham Palace, the Royal Gardens, the Houses

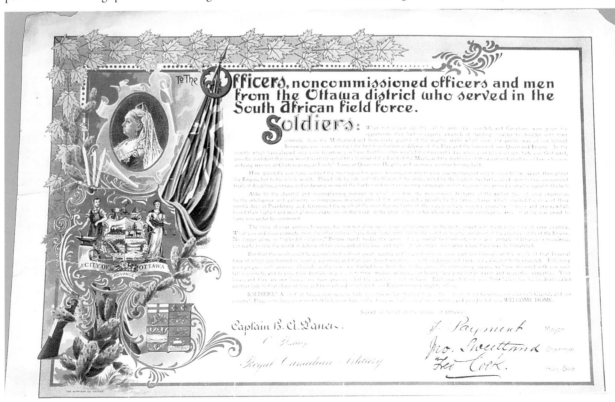

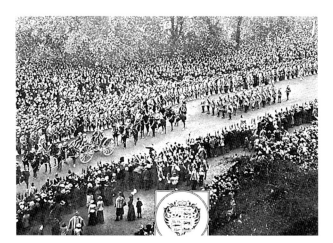

Homecoming ceremony

of Parliament, Portsmouth, Whale Island, Brighton, and Woolwich; a church service at Saint Paul's Cathedral, Lord Strathcona's Canada Club banquet, the Duke of Argyll and Princess Louise's luncheon at Kensington Palace, Lord and Lady Aberdeen's banquet, and the Borough of Kensington's town hall banquet, all with their patriotic music, toasts, interminable speeches and lavish praise.

Not all men followed the full program. A number took leaves to visit English friends and relatives. At least eight men received furlough in England. None, however, disputed the warmth and generosity of the welcoming committee, which treated them as though they "were the eighth wonder of the world."[111]

It was almost with a sense of relief that the Canadians left London for Liverpool to board the *Lake Champlain* for Halifax. Not to be outdone by London, Liverpool's streets were full of noisy, cheering spectators as the Canadians marched to the city hall, where the Mayor presided over a sumptuous luncheon. According to Otter, the climax of the demonstration came at the Exchange, where its members went "wild with enthusiasm," greeting the men with thunderous applause and rousing renditions of "God Save the Queen" and "The Maple Leaf Forever" — all four verses!

Two days before Christmas, 181 jubilant officers and men disembarked at Halifax Harbour for a reception similar to that proffered their regimental comrades. As soon as they were paid and discharged, they were bundled onto trains, determined to reach their homes by Christmas. In their pockets men carried, on average, eighty dollars in pay, or about 38% of their total earnings. At home, their communities often supplemented the amount. For example, each New Brunswick man received an additional $152.[112] Many communities organized elaborate parades, banquets and receptions to welcome their local heroes.

It was a pleasant way to end a service marked by the horrors of combat, disease, privation, monotony and regimental conflict and dissension. The men's inexperience, the confusion and disorganization of their early months in South Africa, the fact that they were foot soldiers in a highly mobile war, together with weak and ineffectual leadership had conspired to make their service especially difficult. In time, these darker experiences would fade into more fanciful recollections of endurance, adventure, comradeship and patriotism.

Medals and ceremonies honour the brave

10

FIGHTING THE NEXT WAR

Subsequent contingents' war experience reaffirmed the Royal Canadians' sense of themselves as a distinctive community within the imperial family. Their experience also made many determined to fight the next war only under senior Canadian officers.

Black Week, that week of British disasters in mid-December 1899, had turned the South African War into Canada's war. Britain's devastating defeats shook Canada's complacent confidence in Britain's arms. The Montreal *Star* spoke for all when it wrote: "If England's power were shattered, Canada might…become an easy prey to one of the great powers…millions should not weigh in the balance, for if England is crushed, Canada is lost….This is our war."[113] French Canada's secular and clerical elite agreed. Persons formerly indifferent or opposed to Canada's participation revised their views. After Black Week, a Canadian consensus emerged committed to Canadian participation, one that crossed linguistic lines.

The War Office's post–Black Week request for a second contingent met with an instant, positive response from the Canadian government, the public and willing volunteers.

The British not only needed more men, but small, company-sized, mobile units composed of men who could ride and shoot and beat the Boers on their own terms.

Recruited immediately after Black Week, Canada's second contingent, however, was a unit in name only. Effectively it operated as three distinct units: two battalions of mounted rifles, entitled the 1st Battalion Canadian Mounted Rifles, and the 2nd Battalion Canadian Mounted Rifles; and a brigade division of field artillery (equivalent to a field regiment of artillery). Altogether it was a contingent of 1,200 men. (In August 1900 when the 1st Canadian Mounted Rifles was re-designated the Royal Canadian Dragoons, to retain its association with the Permanent Canadian Militia, the 2nd Canadian Mounted Rifles became the 1st Canadian Mounted Rifles! (CMR) To avoid confusion, this text will use the August re-designation.)

Although the public painted the second contingent as rough-riding Canadian frontiersmen, only the CMR resembled this popular image. Recruited in western Canada from the ranks of police, ranchers and farm labourers, about 56% were British-born. First known as Herchmer's Horsemen, it was commanded by Lieutenant Laurence Herchmer, a fifty-

Ammunition

Major Evans

nine-year-old, British-born army man, a Tory who had been Commissioner of the North West Mounted Police for thirteen years. Herchmer was a poor choice: slow, harsh and often confused. In South Africa he was relieved of his command and replaced by Major Thomas Dixon Evans, a forty-one-year-old career soldier and veteran of the Northwest Rebellion and the Yukon Field Force. The controversial decision deeply divided the battalion, pitching policemen against militiamen, and was a source of dispute for years to come.

In contrast, the Royal Canadian Dragoons were recruited in eastern and central Canada from the ranks of young white- and blue-collar workers in the Canadian Militia. Most came from cavalry units and were similar in social composition to the men of the Royal Canadians. Their Commanding Officer, Lieutenant-Colonel François Lessard, was a thirty-nine-year-old officer from the Permanent Militia, a diligent, popular officer who had been attached to the Royal Canadians "for special duty," and anxiously awaited his battalion's arrival in South Africa.

The three batteries of the Royal Canadian Field Artillery, designated A, B, and C Batteries, were also recruited in eastern and central Canada from among young, white- and blue-collar urban workers. They were men with military experience and a reasonably good knowledge of their weapons. The British had requested only mounted rifles, but the Canadian military authorities had insisted on sending artillery, since they considered the Canadian artillery their best-trained and best-equipped arm. There was no question of who would command the artillery: Lieutenant-Colonel Charles W. Drury, the popular and competent "father" of the Canadian artillery. He had been attached to the Royal Canadians "for special

duty," and was delighted to assume command of his artillery upon its arrival in Cape Town.

As a temporary unit of the Canadian militia, the second contingent's terms of service, recruitment, equipment, transportation, dispatch and public reception closely resembled those of the first. But since the contingent was recruited in the dead of winter, public demonstrations were more constrained. Official departure ceremonies at Halifax were also more modest; in Halifax the highest-ranking national figure was the Minister of Militia.

Despite the weather, whenever time, temperatures and local resources permitted, crowds gathered at rail stations along the route to cheer, feed and view their soldiers, demonstrations that some enthusiasts claimed surpassed those of the first contingent.[114] 'Herchmer's Horse' enjoyed a particularly warm reception in Ottawa where the Governor-General, who had taken a special interest in its recruitment, had arranged an impressive ceremony on Parliament Hill with Laurier and most of his Cabinet. In Quebec City, snowshoed townsmen bearing torches formed a civilian guard of honour as their local troop of Dragoons marched through cheering crowds to the train station. The public no longer regarded the war as a picnic, a schoolboy's frolic, but as a serious challenge to imperial power and Canada's security.

The most striking difference between recruiting the first and second contingents was the need to purchase, brand, shoe and un-shoe, equip, feed, transport and care for over one thousand horses. Another peculiar feature of the dispatch of

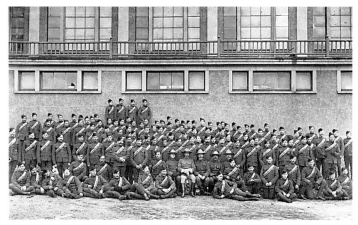

Canadian Mounted Rifles

The Laurentian *sets sail*

the second contingent was the organization of a five-man postal detachment, a project strongly backed by the imperial enthusiast, William Mulock, the Canadian Postmaster General. The Royal Canadian Dragoons, the Canadian Mounted Rifles, the Canadian Field Artillery and Strathcona's Horse appreciated the efficient and cooperative service dispensed by this small detachment, an assessment shared by their British superiors. Similarly, in January 1900 the Canadian government recruited, equipped and transported to South Africa twenty-three artificers, blacksmiths, shoemakers, saddlers and wheelwrights, to support the horse-powered British Army.

The second contingent's immediate challenge, however, was its shipment to South Africa in instalments. Three vessels were commissioned to accommodate the second contingent's men and horses: the *Laurentian*, the *Pomeranian* and the *Milwaukee*. Transportation costs accounted for about 42% of the Canadian government's total expenditure of $1,953,827 on Canada's first two contingents. The scarcity of appropriate, short-term sea transport however obliged the military authorities to send the second contingent by instalments; altogether five weeks separated the arrival of the first and the last shipment of troops.

Life aboard the three vessels followed a familiar pattern. Although all faced a rigorous military regime of meals, fatigues, drills, rifle practice, lectures and watch duty, none endured the regimentation Otter had prescribed for his men. Starkly different from the Royal Canadians' routine, however,

was the disagreeable task of stable duty: watering, feeding and cleaning the horses, disposing of the manure over the ship's side and spreading fresh sawdust and straw. As the ship approached the equator, the stench in the Lower deck's close confines became overwhelming. Fallen horses had to be raised, sick horses tended, and since horse deaths were frequent, their carcasses had to be cut out of their stalls and hoisted overboard.

Despite the number of cavalrymen in their ranks, the CMR and the Dragoons were mounted rifles or mounted infantry, who served as the advance guard's eyes and ears, as scouts, pathfinders, reconnaissance and a column's screen. They rode in extended order, often three hundred yards apart, some two thousand yards ahead of the main force. They examined every building, kopje and ravine and stopped every person and examined passes. Often they went forward to draw out the enemy or detect its whereabouts. Their most tedious task was rearguard duty, protecting the supply lines and rounding up stragglers. Their basic unit was a four-man group. In battle, all four men dismounted; one man served as horse holder out of range of enemy fire, while the others went forward and fought as infantry.

A mounted infantryman's most precious possessions were his rifle and his horse. Their Lee-Enfield was a solid, ten-round, serviceable weapon, though heavy and not effective beyond three thousand yards and not as good as the Boers' Mauser rifle. A trooper's life depended upon a healthy, dependable horse. The Canadians liked their big Canadian

S.S. Pomeranian

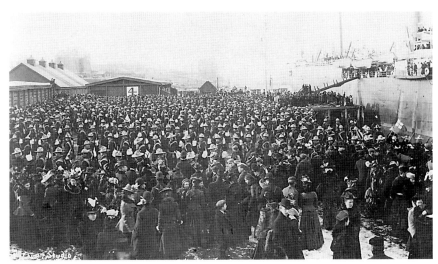

S.S. Milwaukee's departure from Halifax

horses and when they lost them, they preferred the local African breed to the War Office's smaller Argentinean replacement. As a result, they became adept horse thieves. In the opinion of Major-General E.T.H. Hutton, the Canadians were the most notorious horse thieves in the British Army. On one occasion they even stole his horse.

Both mounted units had a machine gun section. Lieutenant Arthur L. "Gat" Howard, the legendary American-born officer who had been named after the gun he operated during the Northwest Rebellion, commanded the Dragoons' section. After his service with Lessard, he commanded a notorious irregular unit called Howard's Canadian Scouts, which after his controversial death did not take prisoners, an offense for which Australia's controversial Breaker Morant paid with his life.

None of the units of the second contingent waited long for a military assignment. When they arrived in Cape Town, the British were savouring news of Roberts' first victories. A day before the *Laurentian* reached Cape Town, the besieged diamond capital, Kimberly, had been freed; and by the time the *Milwaukee* reached port, Bloemfontein was in British hands. Soon after each unit arrived it was deployed, with no regard to the contingent's unity. Nor did the second contingent and the Royal Canadians ever serve together as 'Canada's little army in the field' as many Canadians had hoped.

Since these two contingents were deployed in different theatres of the war, their paths rarely crossed. By February 1900, Roberts commanded a force of some two hundred thousand men (more than equivalent to the entire Boer population); 180,000 were located in the Cape Colony and ready to march to Bloemfontein and Pretoria. Another twenty thousand men (including Canada's Strathcona's Horse) were under the command of Buller, Roberts' discredited predecessor, moving slowly through Natal toward a conjuncture with Roberts' force at Belfast, where they would fight the last formal battle of the war in August 1900. Against them were arrayed no more than fifty thousand Boer commandos.

Herchmer's CMR and Drury's D Battery were attached immediately to Colonel Charles Parson's strenuous but futile six-week Karoo expedition to suppress a Boer rebellion in the Prieska district of Cape Colony. This seven-hundred-mile expedition, over difficult terrain, in inclement weather, and under very trying circumstances, proved a severe trial. Only one shot was fired in anger: ten miles short of their return rendezvous, a picket in D Battery fired at a man who rode to a kraal, tethered his horse, and crept too close to the horses. Nonetheless this expedition proved a severe test of endurance, for some men "the hardest march of the war,"[115] and one in which the CMR leadership failed. It was during this excursion that Herchmer was sent to the Cape on 'sick' leave, and replaced by Evans.

Although all units of Canada's second contingent were deployed quickly, the gun-

Karoo campaigners

Mauser rifles

ners' war proved largely a tedious war against disease and boredom. Divided, dispersed and underutilized, Canada's 'best arm' never had a chance to prove its worth. Many recruits who left their civilian employment for adventure and excitement soon found themselves consigned to the monotonous routine of line-of-communication duty at Kimberly, Warrenton and Vryburg. Posted to the Orange River district shortly after the Karoo campaign, Drury's D and E Batteries spent their time guarding rails, telegraph lines and supply lines, a routine broken only by the occasional rebel-chasing venture into Griqualand West and Bechuanaland. These were slow, cumbersome, poorly-led efforts to capture skilful, elusive Boer commandos, take a few prisoners and 'free' a town, only to have it reoccupied as soon as the British disappeared.

Compass

At Faber's Put, E Battery fought its first battle, the first of only seven engagements during the war.

C Battery, the gunners' last battery to reach South Africa, was its most active, their most celebrated assignment being their march to the relief of Mafeking. Soon after C Battery reached Cape Town, it joined Major-General Frederick Carrington's Rhodesian Field Force in a six-week circuitous expedition from Beira through Bulawayo to relieve the celebrated northern Cape trading post of Mafeking, defended dramatically by Colonel Robert Baden-Powell, a display that captured the public's imagination. On 16 May 1900, at Sanie Station, C Battery briefly engaged the Boer gunners. In honour of their contribution to the relief of Mafeking, "Canada" became the password for entry into the liberated fortress that first night.

Subsequently, C Battery remained with Colonel H.C.O. Plumer in the northwestern Transvaal for the remainder of its service in South Africa, engaged in frustrating efforts to pacify the area. At first, the British established a network of small garrisons to police and disarm the inhabitants. To obtain this objective, the Canadians were posted to Rustenburg, where they built four bastions known as Fort Canada, each bastion named after artillery postings in Canada: Kingston, Toronto, Hamilton and Winnipeg.

But when the Boers showed no sign of weakening, and the British realized that they had become semi-captives of their garrisons, increasingly an object of attack, they devised a more offensive strategy, rounding up suspects and burning crops and farms. Although C Battery served in a number of these engagements, when their service in South Africa ended they left behind them an empty legacy: a northwestern Transvaal scarcely less pacified than it had been six months before. This was not the war they had come to fight.

Separated from their comrades, the gunners tired quickly of their perfunctory duties of drills, fatigues, road construction and caring for horses. At populous posts, civilians opened rooms where men could read, write and buy cakes and coffee.

Regular church services and occasional sports contests provided some relief, and alarms, rumours and the occasional sniping broke the monotony of camp life. But the rest of the time the gunners had little to do but complain, endure lice and dust storms, drink and seek female company.

Handgun

The second contingent's two mounted battalions, however, suffered relatively little from boredom. Shortly after the CMR returned from the Karoo campaign, it joined the Dragoons at Bloemfontein. There they joined Brigadier-General E.A. Alderson's Mounted Infantry Corps, assigned to Major-General E.T.H. Hutton's 1st Mounted Infantry Brigade. Hutton was the former General Officer of the Canadian Militia, who had been removed by the Canadian government for insubordination and whom the British sent to South Africa to command a 'colonial' brigade.

Several days after the Canadians joined Hutton's brigade, they began their march to Pretoria, following the right side of the rail. Their compatriots, the Royal Canadians, were on the left. Their first engagement occurred at Brandfort, where the (in)famous Canadian scout, Charlie Ross, was the first to enter the town. Other battles followed on the Vet River, and on the Zand River.

On the Vet the CMR and the Dragoons distinguished themselves for their initiative and courage. Two of the Dragoons' very able lieutenants, Richard E. Turner from Quebec City, whose brother was wounded on Bloody Sunday, and Harold Borden were mentioned in dispatches. A five-day march brought them to Kroonstad, the Orange Free State's seat of government following the British occupation of Bloemfontein. At the Vaal River they were obliged to fight a disciplined battle

Fanciful representation of Boers' violation of the white flag (note the Red Cross on his arm)

to dislodge their opponents. One more skirmish and the mounted battalions entered Pretoria, where they expected to celebrate the war's end.

The conventional war may have ended, but the dirty war was about to begin. The new war required mounted troops for escort, search and reconnaissance, to counter the Boers' hit-and-run tactics.

After the British occupation of Pretoria, as the army restocked, reorganized and planned its next moves, the value of Canada's mounted battalions was far from apparent. During this period of uncertainty and confusion, the CMR were more fortunate than the Dragoons. After their deployment at Diamond Hills, just outside Pretoria, the CMR were consigned to line of communication duty on the Koonstad-Vereeniging railway.

Deployed in small, autonomous groups along the rail line, mounted men (in contrast to infantry and artillery soldiers) possessed mobility and personal freedom, and the possibility of personal adventures. Looting or liaisons with civilians were explained in terms of taking a wrong turn! Occasionally they fought serious engagements. One tragic engagement that deserves greater recognition occurred at Katsbosh on 22 June 1900, where a brave four-man guard composed of men from Pincher Creek fought to the death.

Meanwhile the Dragoons vegetated at Deerdepoort, coping with disease and boredom, many without horses. British career officers sought to strengthen their forces by shamelessly raiding men from other units. Some Dragoons succumbed to the temptation of competing military and policing opportunities. Those who remained undertook occasional excursions to clear the surrounding area of snipers and commandos.

More active service followed Roberts' resumption of his northwestern Transvaal campaign, an operation designed to cut the Boers' last remaining rail line to the sea via Komati Poort through Portuguese territory to Lourenco Marquess. In preparation for this campaign, Canada's two mounted battalions were sent to help clear the Boers from Tigerpoort, Witpoort and Kafferspruit. This successful but costly engagement claimed the lives of two of the Dragoons' popular lieutenants, J.E. Burch and Harold Borden, the only son of Canada's Minister of Militia. In a moving torchlight service the next evening the two men were buried near a farm at Rietvlei (they were later re-interred at Braamfontein, Johannesburg).

Borden memorial

The death of the two young officers deeply affected the battalion and caused great public sorrow. One of Lessard's most competent, reliable lieutenants, Borden had volunteered against his father's advice. Before leaving home he had promised that he would never ask his men to do anything he would not do himself; and he had been as good as his word. Twice before Borden's death, Hutton, who had quarrelled publicly with Borden's father, had brought "Lieutenant Borden to the Commander-in-Chief's notice for intrepid and gallant conduct."[116]

Borden's prominence fed various fanciful stories of the circumstances surrounding his death. According to one unsubstantiated tale, an Irish-American who had been fighting with the Boers had shot Borden; subsequently the Canadians had captured and handed him over to the Irish Fusiliers, who were fighting alongside the Canadians, and the outraged Fusiliers murdered the American sniper.

When the British halted their march at Middelburg on 25

July 1900 to pursue De Wet, Canada's mounted battalions were consigned to patrol duty at Blankfontein, Aasvogel, Nooitgedacht, Wonderfontein and Belfast. Here they remained for the rest of the war, engaged in bitter skirmishes with roving Boer commandos and sharpshooters. Here too they participated in the British Army's increasingly distasteful scorched earth policy, herding women and children into concentration camps and burning their crops and farms. The practice was designed to force the Boer soldiers from the camouflage of their farms and into the field, but some of the Canadian farm boys found the activity especially unpleasant.

It was during one of these missions that Canadian troops fought one of their most spectacular battles of the war, at Liliefontein. In the early morning darkness of 6 November 1900, the Canadians left their station at Belfast under the direction of Smith-Dorrien to destroy farms suspected of harbouring rail saboteurs and to break up commandos at Carolina and Witkloof.

Four hours out of Belfast the Boers appeared, determined to slow their progress. Faced by Boer opposition, the British advance guard pushed forward from ridge to ridge toward Van Wyk's Vlei. In charge of one of the guns was Lieutenant E.W.B. Morrison (future author of *With The Guns In South Africa*). Morrison's guns were especially accurate, as was Sergeant Edward Holland, a young Ottawa graduate of Lisgar Collegiate in charge of Gat Howard's Colt. The men in other units observing the battle applauded. By noon the Boers had been driven back to Witkloof.

Meanwhile the Boers' Carolina Commandos took up their well-chosen positions on a steep, rocky ridge along the Komati River from Witkloof to Liliefontein. Although Lessard's Dragoons and four British infantry companies attempted to climb the ridge and silence the Boers, it took

Morrison's gunners and Holland's Colt to dampen the Boer fire and permit the British artillery to reach the top and cover the infantry's climb. Morrison was so successful that Smith-Dorrien "rode up and personally complimented" the Canadian gunners. Put to the test, Canada's "best arm" had not failed.

Gatling gun

Smith-Dorrien had decided to return to Belfast. Although the British possessed sufficient supplies and probably twice as many men as the Boers, they lacked mobility, encumbered by their interminable supply wagons. Smith-Dorrien had decided not to attempt what he might not accomplish. As yesterday's advance guard, the Canadians

Although the British incurred twenty-six casualties, they were unable to dislodge the Carolina Commandos. To break the deadlock, Smith-Dorrien ordered Lessard's Dragoons and two British companies to cut off the Commandos' retreat along the Carolina road. Once the Boers appreciated the British intent, they evacuated their positions. By 4:00 p.m. the battle was over, and the road to Carolina was open. The British camped on two adjoining farms at Liliefontein and Goedehoop, within sight of the Komati River and in command of the Carolina road. During the evening both sides took counsel.

All afternoon and early evening the Boers lit signal fires to recall the men who had quit military service temporarily for planting season. Convinced that the British would move on to Carolina, the Boers decided to imitate the British entrapment tactic of the previous day. The Carolina Commandos' General J.C. Fourie and his second-in-command, Commandant H.R. Prinsloo, would make a frontal attack on Liliefontein, while General Jans Grobler and a party from another commando unit drove the British into a trap.

The Boers, however, had misread British intentions:

would serve as rearguard, to protect the retreating supply wagons.

Early the next morning, Evans' CMR were the first to see action. Spotting Fourie's men moving toward a strategic ridge, Evans' horsemen staged a spectacular and successful two-mile race to secure the ridge. From there they forced the Boers to seek security on the other side of the valley, from which the CMR protected the large British convoy until it lumbered to safety some two miles away; then the CMR returned to the main body of the column.

Meanwhile, Smith-Dorrien ordered an infantry company and a squadron of cavalry to seize the high ground at Van Wyk's Vlei, leaving the Dragoons, three companies of British infantry and Morrison's two guns, "very weak in numbers compared to the column," to protect the rearguard.[117] Lessard, however, was ready for the challenge, a plan he explained carefully to his officers, while the men rested in the grass and waited for the last wagon to lumber out of the camp.

Lessard planned to move by stages: the Dragoons, the infantry, and the guns were to hold the last ridge until the transport wagons had reached the next one. Then the infantry would move forward and cover the guns as they retired one at a time, the second covering the first. Once the guns had reached the ridge and had begun to fire, the Dragoons were to gallop forward in extended order, low in their saddles under the protection of the guns. The success of the plan depended on timing, skill and luck.

As soon as the CMR returned to the main column, Fourie's men, frustrated by their failure to seize the ridge, wreaked their vengeance on Lessard's rearguard. The appearance of another commando unit on the horizon persuaded Lessard to seek reinforcements, and Evans' CMR immediately covered Lessard's left flank.

Lessard was superb, courageous, decisive, cool and insistent. During the worst of the battle he rode along the ridge, maintaining a clear overview of the engagement, anticipating moves, devising tactics, reassigning troops to shore up weak defences, making difficult decisions and encouraging the men. When Lessard saw that Lieutenant H.Z.C. Cockburn's men were in serious trouble, he immediately ordered Morrison to take his gun to Cockburn's assistance. Racing a mile or more across the ridge, Morrison's shells slowed but failed to stop the tide of Boer horsemen. Morrison had fired no more than twelve rounds when Lessard galloped toward him, ordering Morrison to save his guns. A glance at his left rear convinced Morrison of the order's urgency: Boer reinforcements were coming on in numbers that could not be stopped.

While Morrison sought the safety of the next ridge, Cockburn's men were left unprotected to face the stampede. All knew that the guns must be saved. To give Morrison time, Cockburn threw the rest of his troops against the enemy. Although the men knew the outcome, "not a man hesitated."[118] Their mission accomplished, Cockburn and his troops now completely surrounded, were taken prisoner.

As soon as Morrison's gun had been saved, Lessard collected additional men to shore up another wavering line. There, Corporal Thomas Kerr, who was in charge of Morrison's other gun, was on his way to the next ridge under the protection of Holland's Colt. The Boers, having captured large quantities of ammunition, needed the Canadians' guns.

Morrison's exhausted artillery horses, however, were hav-

ing trouble getting the guns to the crest of the ridge. They had slowed down to a walk. About one-third of the way from the crest, with the Boer horsemen only twelve hundred yards away, Morrison saw no alternative but to halt and turn his guns on the tide of horsemen. While he managed to scatter some parties with shrapnel and case shot, he failed to stop the onslaught.

Things seemed desperate. One of Morrison's guns was well ahead of the other, and Morrison feared that Holland's Colt's temporary silence meant that it had been captured. Morrison had not reckoned on Holland's courage and intelligence. Standing off his pursuers until they were within two hundred yards of his Colt, Holland had simply unscrewed its barrel from the carriage, put it under his arm and galloped off as he and Gat Howard had done at Diamond Hills. Encouraged by Holland's daring, Morrison made one more effort to reach the top and secure the protection of the infantry's rifles. The gunners dismounted and the horses, rested by the brief stop, broke "into a trot with the gunners running alongside pulling on the traces."[119]

Still, Morrison's guns were far from safe. Much to Morrison's anger, when his gunners almost reached the protection of the British infantry, the British regular troops broke and ran, leaving Canada's citizen soldiers to their fate. With the Boers moving ever closer and one of his artillery horses wounded, Morrison sent his only mounted escort to seek Lessard's assistance.

Morrison's request for assistance, however, never reached Lessard. His messenger met Turner on the way, and although Turner had been wounded, he rallied about twelve men, using his wound "as an example to the men" and appealing to their pride: "Never let it be said," he shouted, "that Canadians let their guns be captured."[120] He then placed himself and them in whatever slight shelter they could find between Morrison's guns and the charging Boer horsemen, and waited.

Fourie had decided that they would never have a better opportunity to take the guns. Evans' CMR were now visible on the next ridge. Fourie and Prinsloo raced forward with a hundred others, firing from their saddles, a spectacle that reminded Canadians of a Wild West show. In their excitement they had failed to detect Turner's ambush until it was too late. Fourie was the first to fall, followed by Prinsloo.

By 2:00 p.m. the Battle of Liliefontein was all but over. Turner had saved the guns. As the guns escaped over the ridge, Morrison caught up with the British infantry, which had not fired a shot. Morrison asked one of their officers to fire a few rounds until he got his guns into action. "The British officer answered shortly: 'I can do nothing' and they went faster over the crest of the ridge." There were, Morrison scornfully recalled, "three companies of them, as many if not more than all the force we had in the fight."[121]

Turner's ambush had cost the Canadians casualties. Turner himself was wounded in the neck and Sergeant Nelson Builder was mortally wounded. Totally surrounded, those in Turner's party who could not escape surrendered and joined Cockburn's men; together they were about sixteen prisoners in all. That evening all were released. The Boers had no provisions to care for prisoners. During their captivity, the Canadians were exceptionally well-treated. The Boers cared for the Canadian wounded until the British ambulances arrived. They bore the Canadians no ill: indeed they seemed to like "the Canadians, and even asked some of our men if they would join them." The Canadians were equally impressed with their captors: "a very superior lot…splendidly mounted, well dressed, and most of them with Kaffir servants."[122] Smith-Dorrien later thanked the Boers for their generous treatment of the Canadians.

News of the Canadians' exploits preceded them. Upon their arrival in Belfast the next morning, a trainload of British Tommies cheered them. Smith-Dorrien, the clever wordsmith, described the Canadian repulse of the final Boer charge as "an event unprecedented in this war" and declared that he had "no praise too high for the devoted gallantry" the Canadians "showed in keeping the enemy off the infantry and convoy."[123] Turner, Cockburn and Holland received a Victoria Cross; an unprecedented number of Canadians to have received the award in one engagement. Had Builder lived, Smith-Dorrien would have recommended him as well. Morrison received the Distinguished Service Order and Private William Albert Knisley, who had rescued his chum under fire, obtained the Distinguished Conduct Medal.

No flood of telegrams from dignitaries and public bodies greeted the Liliefontein heroes. After the British occupation of Pretoria, the Canadian reporters had gone home. Moreover, a close scrutiny of the British infantry's behaviour might have raised some embarrassing questions. The experience, however, was not lost on Canada's citizen soldiers. They were proud of their performance. They knew that they had fought a coordinated, intelligent, courageous battle, and were proud that they had done so as a Canadian unit, deserted by the British infantry. Significantly outnumbered, the Canadian citizen soldiers had engaged the Boers on their own terrain, employed their own tactics, and had beaten them and won their respect. Although Liliefontein possessed neither strategic nor symbolic importance, the Canadians had saved their guns, the British baggage and supply wagons and many casualties among the British infantry. Best of all, for quiet patriots like Morrison, the battle at Liliefontein raised the hope "that in the next war the Canadian troops would be formed in one division."[124] Morrison, Turner and others lived to serve in that World War I division.

11

NO SURRENDER

Two months before the war ended on 31 May 1902, at Harts River, Canadian troops fought another spectacular rearguard battle, one of the three most celebrated Canadian engagements of the war. This second–most–costly Canadian battle was marked by acts of extraordinary heroism, and became the subject of patriotic commemoration in picture, bronze and verse. For years, veterans of the Battle of Harts River, like their compatriots from Paardeberg and Liliefontein, gathered annually to remember and celebrate this event. Since they possessed no regimental link to the Canadian Militia, their commemoration faded with the battle's last survivors.

Officers of Strathcona's Horse

Well before their celebrated battle, Canada raised two other units for service in South Africa. Two weeks after Black Week, while the Canadian government was recruiting men for the second contingent, Canada's wealthy and powerful High Commissioner to London, Lord Strathcona, offered to finance the recruitment, equipment, transport and partial payment of wages of a five-hundred-man battalion of scouts.

Although a temporary unit of the British Army, Strathcona's scouts were to be recruited in the Canadian Northwest by Canada's Militia Department. Named in honour of their benevolent sponsor, the Lord Strathcona's Horse's commander was Colonel Samuel B. Steele, the legendary fifty-one-year-old superintendent of the North West Mounted Police, an energetic, shrewd and able manager of men and a meticulous administrator who had no time for the stupidities of barrack square drill.

Dramatized representation of the Boers versus Strathcona's Horse

The public viewed Lord Strathcona's Horse as a body of sturdy roughriders of the plain, self-reliant, western frontiersmen who could "tell the time by a glance of the sun, to whom the trees and grasses were true compasses and who regarded the rifle as their constant companions." The reality was somewhat more mundane. They were raised in the Northwest and British Columbia, a month after the CMR recruiters had raked the area for recruits. Many of the good, mobile, obvious prospects had enrolled in Herchmer's unit. Nonetheless, the social composition of Strathcona's three-squadron battalion resembled the CMR more than any other Canadian unit: policemen, ranchers, farmers, farm hands and packers, except that the men in Strathcona's Horse tended to be older and more were British-born. Among them were remittance men, a few with titles.[125]

Ironically, while Otter attempted to efface his battalion's Canadian character, the unit that possessed the highest number of Canadian-born, Steele shrewdly cultivated a Canadian image for his scouts: Canadian pioneers who had lived "in the fastness of the Wild West," a romantic image appreciated by the British higher command and which Steele never hesitated to use to his unit's advantage.

Lord Strathcona's Horse faced many challenges: the recruitment and subsequent death from disease of many of their horses, as well as the delay in their dispatch to and deployment in South Africa. By the time Strathcona's Horse was ordered into action, Pretoria had been occupied. In the subsequent reorganization, Strathcona's Horse was consigned to General Sir Redvers Buller's Natal Field Force. Buller's object was to join Roberts' forces at Belfast, where together they would fight the last formal set battle of the war.

Buller, who had served in Canada during the Red River expedition, warmly welcomed the Canadians to his slow-moving force. As Buller's scouts, Strathcona's Horse fought skirmishes, performed outpost and escort duty and engaged in battles at Platkop, Holgatefontein, Standerton, Amersfoort, Ralfontein and Belfast-Bergendal. It was during a costly and unfortunate skirmish at Standerton on 5 July that Sergeant Arthur Richardson earned Canada's first Victoria Cross of the war. Richardson had ridden back under heavy crossfire to pick up a horseless wounded comrade and bring him to safety.

After the battle of Belfast-Bergendal, Strathcona's Horse joined Lord Dundonald's 3rd Mounted Brigade, fought its way to Lydenberg and subsequently pursued Louis Botha's Commando. Soon after the Lydenberg campaign, in early

Boer War figurine

October 1900 when Lord Dundonald's Brigade was broken up, the Canadians were ordered to Pretoria to await a new assignment. Many were convinced that they were on their

way home.

While they waited at Machadodorp for a train to Pretoria, the

men camped on either side of the rail, unprotected from the rain, thunder and lightning, relaxed and in a celebratory mood. Officers had difficulty maintaining order among the restless men. Some made no effort to do so, especially after Steele's departure for Pretoria. Damp, cold, bored and anticipating their immediate release from service, the men wanted alcohol. The more entrepreneurial resorted to a familiar ruse. They marched to the quartermaster's store and forged the signature of Steele's second-in-command, Major Robert Belcher; shortly they became drunk, noisy and disorderly, shouting and firing their revolvers in the air. The British Provost Marshal, a British Major and a couple of mounted police came to investigate. As the Provost stooped to examine a crude, suspicious looking "bivouac with a light in it and in which a sergeant and a corporal were making merry with a bottle full of rum," one of the Canadians came up behind the Provost and "fired his revolver close to each side of his head." In the dark and the confusion the culprit could not be identified.

The shaken Provost ordered several companies of British infantry to surround the Canadian squadron and parade the merrymakers. The Canadians were marched for several hours until they sobered up. The next day the authorities investigated the affair but took no action since "we were irregular

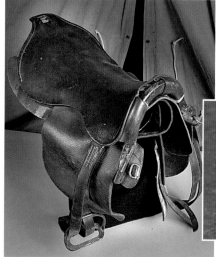

Strathcona's Horse saddle and pin

troops and our Colonel was away."[126] Needless to say, this incident received no publicity in Canada.

Much to their disappointment, the merrymakers were not bound for home but reassigned to the southwestern Transvaal, for a time at Frederikstad and Potchefstroom under the command of Colonel H.T. Hicks. Confined to these locations for several weeks, the battalion was plagued by enteric and dysentery,

Troops on the veldt

and employed in various tasks: searching homes, capturing armed men, confiscating cattle and, most hateful of all, herding women and children into concentration camps and burning their farms; in Steele's view this was a disagreeable work totally unsuited to his unit.[127]

Although more active, their reassignment to Major-General Charles Knox's command in the southeastern Free State was not much more satisfactory. Their new assignment's objective was to track and capture the ever-elusive General De Wet, a lethargic, disorganized expedition that diminished Steele's declining respect for British military leadership. After one year's service, the Strathcona's Horse, like the remainder of Otter's Royal Canadians, returned to Canada via London, where they confronted elaborate receptions, as much a tribute to Strathcona's standing in London as to his regiment's solid service record.

Lord Strathcona's Horse were equally well-received at home. Its regimental esprit de corps was never more apparent than during its demobilization. The men's reluctance to see the unit break up was a tribute to its Commanding Officer's ability to lead a diverse, rowdy body of men through difficult times. It also provided an occasion for Steele to affirm his faith in Canada and its citizen soldiers. In an emotional final address, Steele admonished his men: "Boys, never forget that you are Canadians and that Canada, as a country, has no supe-rior in the wide world," and above all be "proud of being a Canadian. Remember that you are Canadians first. Remember Canada."[128] From a Commanding Officer of a very 'British' unit, and from a man who was very critical of British military leadership, Steele's words were heavy with meaning.

Strathcona's Horse served in South Africa contemporaneously with the Royal Canadians and the second contingent's units, though in different theatres. After their return, from January 1901 until March 1902, Canada had no men in South Africa except for those who joined British irregular units, such as the Howard's Canadian Scouts, or the Canadians in the South African Constabulary.

The name, leadership, reputation and concentration of the Canadians in Howard's Canadian Scouts gave them a large audience in Canada. The Canadian Scouts had been raised in December 1900 by Major "Gat" Howard, the commander of Lessard's machine-gun section, an unorthodox character whose exploits won him mention in dispatches and an almost folkloric reputation among senior British officers. Indeed, he served as the model for Rudyard Kipling's short story, "The Captive," later published in *Traffics and Discoveries* (London, 1928). Given his charismatic reputation, Howard had no difficulty raising a company of short service, 'irregular' scouts from the ranks of the Canadian veterans, a force armed with six Colt guns and a pom-pom.

Although he had not confined his recruitment to Canadian troops, about eighty-five of his initial 107 men were Canadian veterans, more than two-thirds from the ranks of the second contingent's underemployed artillery. Among these were men such as "Casey" Callaghan, R.H. Ryan and Charlie Ross, himself a remarkable character who subsequently succeeded Howard as the Scouts' commander.[129] As the dirty war continued and Kitchener became more desperate to end the war and leave South Africa for a plum position in India, the Canadian Scouts extended their service from six months until the war's end, and expanded well beyond a company-sized unit.

With time, attrition and expansion, the Scouts recruited adventurers from many countries, including a squadron of Afrikaners. Nonetheless, the Scouts retained their Canadian name, insignia and a disproportionate component of Canadian officers. The insignia consisted of a plain maple leaf with three chevrons, since all but a tiny number were 'sergeants,' Howard supposedly making up the difference between a trooper's and a sergeant's pay.[130]

Assigned to General E.A.H. Alderson's Infantry, the Scouts began action in January 1901, working in

Major "Gat" Howard

small groups, often as a screen for the main force. They quickly earned a reputation for aggressive, fearless, foolhardy ventures, and costly casualty counts. Among their casualties was their fifty-five-year-old commander. On 17 February, Howard and his orderly Sergeant Richard Northway, a thirty-year-old English-born CMR veteran, were found dead. The circumstances of their deaths remain a subject of speculation. One story alleged that the Boers had ambushed Howard and his party from behind four wagons. Another affirmed that Howard had surrendered and his captors had murdered him.

The Canadian Scouts were convinced that their commander had been captured, then "foully murdered," his body pumped full of bullets, his "murderers" laughing as they watched him die. When the Scouts located their commander's body, and before they wrapped him in sheets to be returned to the base camp, Howard's close friend and second-in-command, Charlie Ross, gathered his men around Howard's body and ordered them to raise their right hand and swear that they

would "never take another Boer prisoner." According to one participant, "Somewhere between three hundred and four hundred Boers died to pay" for Howard's death.[131] Those who took the oath continued to wear a black feather in their hat as a token of their pledge.

Ross immediately assumed command of the Canadian Scouts, a force that soon numbered as many as three hundred. Ross had been born in Australia, came to the United States, served for a time in the North West Mounted Police (NWMP) and during the Riel Rebellion had met Howard. A restless, entrepreneurial man, Ross left the NWMP, spent time in the Yukon and through the good offices of General Hutton went to South Africa to seek employment during the war. When Hutton reached South Africa, he made Ross his Chief Scout and Ross served with distinction. Leaving Hutton, Ross went into a dubious 'business,' reputedly selling goods to both sides.[132] Although the Canadian government had nothing to do with its creation, the Canadian Scouts continued to be seen as part of Canada's contribution to the war.

Canadians from Strathcona's Horse and other units also remained in South Africa to join Lord Baden-Powell's recently-organized South African Constabulary. Men like Steele joined after a brief sojourn at home. A hybrid civilian/military police force of some ten thousand men, the South African Constabulary was conceived by Lord Milner to maintain civil authority in South Africa in the wake of British conquest and occupation. As part of his larger 'final solution' to 'pacify' and 'civilize' South Africa, Milner hoped to induce volunteers to settle there by encouraging the enlistment of married men, providing an opportunity to purchase a farm and insisting on a three-year service contract. To justify its cost, the War Office insisted that the men serve as soldiers during the war. To many Canadian recruits this was the real incentive to volunteer.

The Constabulary's Commanding Officer was Baden-Powell, the hero of Mafeking and future founder of the Boy Scouts, who had commanded Canada's C Battery in the northwestern Transvaal. Baden-Powell had formed a high opinion of Canadian troops and attempted to recruit men whose one-year service contracts had expired. Although some gunners volunteered, most of the 1,200 Canadians who joined his Constabulary were recruited in Canada — about half in western Canada and half in eastern and central Canada. Among them were large numbers of veterans from other contingents, including the Queen's scarf recipient Richard Roland Thompson. From the start, the Canadian government and public resented British attempts to entice Canadians to settle in South Africa at a time when Canada was making great efforts to attract immigrants; efforts to have Steele recruit another thousand men encountered sufficient Canadian opposition to scotch the effort.

Baden-Powell had great confidence in Steele. He placed him in command of one of his four divisions. Inspired by Steele's North West Mounted Police experience, Baden-Powell sought and followed Steele's counsel; consequently this experience played a significant role in shaping the character of the Constabulary. Baden-Powell even envisaged naming Steele as his successor, his one reservation being Steele's weakness for alcohol.

For more than a year, the Canadian constables were the only Canadian military presence in South Africa. This was the period of the dirty war, the guerrilla phase that placed a heavy demand on men, as they constructed and manned blockhouses, escorted convoys and engaged in drives.

In August 1900, the British victory at Belfast-Bergendal cut the Boers' last rail link to the sea and Kruger fled to Holland. In October 1900, Britain annexed the two Boer republics. Thereafter Britain treated those who resisted as rebels, fugitives and outlaws rather than prisoners of war. Convinced that the war was over, Roberts returned to Britain, leaving Kitchener to mop up, an operation that required more time and resources than the British had anticipated — a task in which Kitchener employed increasingly desperate methods.

With no fixed base to defend, the Boers were more mobile and elusive than ever. Organized into marauding bands of men who united into large commandos units and then divided into smaller squads as occasion demanded; the 'bitter enders' were farmers one day and soldiers the next, living on a land they knew intimately, supported by civilians for whose cause they were fighting. Cut off from their normal supply of arms and ammunition, they equipped and helped feed themselves from captured British convoys and abandoned British campsites. Their success in wrecking British transportation and communications, raiding supply depots, capturing cumbersome, well-stocked British supply convoys

Strathcona's Horse officer, Ottawa

Director-General Neilson and officers of Canadian Hospital Corps

and reoccupying poorly defended garrisons made a mockery of British rule and fed the hopes of the 'bitter enders' that they might make British control untenable.

To cope with these guerrilla tactics, the British countered with a scorched earth policy, and constructed chains of block-houses along the rail lines, connected by some six thousand kilometres of barbed wire and telephone communications — each blockhouse manned by four infantrymen or mounted police, often from the South African Constabulary. Similar lines constricted open country, forming large rectangular compartments. These enclosures were then 'swept' by long lines of troops who searched every building, devastated crops, confiscated livestock, burned buildings and herded women, children and old men into concentration camps where almost twenty-eight thousand Boers and some sixteen thousand Blacks died from disease and malnutrition. The object of these 'drives' was "to remove every living person, animal and sustenance-giving plant from the veldt."

In the war to the finish, the women fared much worse than the more mobile male warriors. Left to manage their farms and servants, provisions and shelter the men on commando, women were an easy, sedentary target for British retribution. Witnesses to the destruction of their homes, they were turned out on the veldt to fend for themselves; the women were later herded into concentration camps to face malnutrition, disease and death.

As the British noose tightened, the plight of the Boer civilians became increasingly desperate. Unable to feed prisoners, the Boers stripped the prisoners and released them; so pressed were they for clothing that they stripped the dead as well.

Although Strathcona's Horse and units of the second contingent participated in some of the early scorched earth expeditions, their departure left only the Canadian constables as witnesses and participants in these acts of 'barbarism,' as they were branded by a portion of Britain's Liberal press and Canadians such as Henri Bourassa.

Kitchener's scorched earth strategy required large numbers of men, a requirement made difficult by the departure of colonial troops whose time had expired. To meet this demand, in November 1901 the British government sought additional colonial assistance. Their request met an enthusiastic public reception in Canada where the Tory press had been calling for a greater Canadian presence in South Africa. What the British wanted was a mounted unit of about six hundred men. What they finally accepted was a force of 901 officers and men, under the experienced and capable command of Lieutenant-Colonel T.D.B. Evans, the former officer commanding the 1st CMR. In keeping with Evans' former unit, they were named the 2nd Canadian Mounted Rifles.

The 2nd CMR, the unit that was to fight the famous Harts River battle, was recruited during the closing months of the war, and resembled its namesake in most respects except that it was a temporary unit of the British Army, not obliged to seek permission or accept advice from Ottawa. They were not alone. Lord Strathcona's Horse and four small battalions raised too late for action, the 3rd, 4th, 5th and 6th Canadian Mounted Rifles, were also temporary units of the British Army.

Evans' 2nd CMR was Canada's most cohesive, experienced, and best-led contingent. Composed of six squadrons, half of its men were recruited in western Canada and the rest in central and eastern Canada. About 22% were South African War veterans; sixty-three of the men were from Strathcona's Horse. Among the veterans were men such as Corporal William Knisley, who had won a Distinguished Conduct Medal at Liliefontein; Sergeant John Campbell Perry, who had been wounded in the knee at Paardeberg; Captain J.H. Elmsley, another Liliefontein veteran; Bruce Carruthers, who had resigned his commission to serve as a sergeant with the Dragoons; and Lieutenant Thomas "Casey" Callaghan, who won the Distinguished Service Medal for his service with Evans' 1st CMR and was perhaps the best Canadian scout in the war.

Lieutenant Bruce Carruthers

Anxious to test Canada's medical personnel and equipment, Borden despatched eight nursing sisters and a sixty-four-man Field Hospital under the command of Lieutenant-Colonel Arthur Worthington, a South African veteran of the Royal Canadian Field Artillery. Recruited in January 1902, the 10th Canadian Field Hospital possessed hospital tents, convertible ambulance/transport wagons, water carts, and other hospital equipment and supplies, some of Canadian design or adaptation. During its three-month stint in South Africa with Evans' 2nd CMR, Worthington's unit had ample opportunity to test its organization and equipment and to demonstrate its utility.

Two troop ships conveyed the men and their 1,096 horses to Durban, an unusually long voyage. They were immediately attached to Brigadier-General Walter Kitchener's (the Commander-in-Chief's brother) division, stationed at Klerksdorp in the western Transvaal, one of the war's most active theatres. About a week after the Canadians reached

Durban, General J.H. de la Rey's commando had trapped and captured a British force, including the area's senior British officer, Lord Methuen. During the engagement, sixty-four men had been killed and 110 wounded, a humiliation that Kitchener's division was called to avenge.

On 23 March 1902, three days after they reached Klerksdorp, Evans' men joined a gruelling twenty-three hour 'drive' toward Witpoort, their only battle experience before Harts River. Nothing, however, could have prepared them for what followed. On Good Friday, 28 March, three days after the Canadians' return from Witpoort, Kitchener's sixteen-thousand-man division launched a major offensive. In preparation for the 'drive' early Easter Monday, two of Kitchener's columns, commanded by Colonel S. Cookson, were ordered to establish contact with the Boer commandos. Evans' left wing escorted the slow-moving supply and baggage, while his right wing marched with the main column. Casey Callaghan and his scouts served as advance guard.

At about 10:00 a.m., Callaghan's scouts picked up the trail of a Boer commando force of about five hundred men with two guns and received permission to pursue them. Although Cookson ordered troops forward to support Callaghan, the reinforcements arrived too late. Callaghan's men had fallen into a trap and were ambushed. Two of them were killed and nine wounded.

This was the vanguard of a much larger commando force. Positioned on both sides of the ridges in front of Cookson's 1,800 man advance guard were about 2,500 Boers.

bandolier

Close to his destination near the junction of the Brak Spruit and Harts River, Cookson stopped and waited for his convoys. Unfortunately, he chose a campsite in a valley surrounded by hills. Moreover, he made no provision to scout the surrounding hills, dig trenches or lay down trip lines. He posted only an outer screen of guards along the right and left sides, and two mounted troops to guard the rear of the camp, no more than two hundred men in all, with their four guns and two pom-poms.

Meanwhile the Boers, chronically short of provisions and supplies, waited patiently for the arrival of the British convoys. As soon as the last supply wagon arrived and the Boers had a more accurate estimate of British strength, they unleashed a massive artillery attack on the British left flank, followed by two mounted rifle assaults. Only then did the British dig trenches and set up trip lines.

The Boers concentrated their fire on the prized convoys at the rear. Convinced they could storm the faltering British defences, they charged seven times, circling wildly and shooting from their horses as in a Wild West show. In response to the Boers' sustained pressure, the British ordered their outer guard to withdraw to their inner defences which they did in panic, fleeing directly to the safety of the main camp, leaving Lieutenant Bruce Carruthers and two Canadian troops alone to face the onslaught.

Once the last wagon lumbered into camp, Carruthers and his troop on convoy duty felt they might usefully remain in

Stone breastwork at Sangam, designed to protect troops from observation and enemy fire

the rearguard. He sent Sergeant John Campbell Perry to camp for orders. There the adjutant instructed Carruthers' group to "remain where it was until it was relieved," an order it obeyed implicitly, despite its awful cost.

Shortly after Perry returned, the Boers launched another massive assault. To counterattack, the British mounted infantry deployed 125 rearguard soldiers to protect their left flank, leaving seventy-five men to cope with the rearguard. To fill the gap, Carruthers moved twenty-one of his men to support the beleaguered rearguard. At this point, the Boers attacked. Short of ammunition and greatly outnumbered, the British rearguard panicked and fled, straight through the Canadian lines.

When his men wavered, Carruthers, like Turner at Liliefontein, decided to stem the rout. Dismounting and shouting "no surrender," Carruthers turned to face the onslaught. He shot the first Boer with his revolver at a distance of fifteen paces. With the assistance of Sergeant John Perry, Corporal J.S. Wilkinson, Lance Corporal John Charles Bond, a veteran of the 2nd contingent's artillery and Private S. McCall, Carruthers rallied his men, dismounted them and grouped them into a half-moon formation to face the enemy. Sergeant Edwin Hodgins and ten of his men followed suit. Together, the Canadians lay prone in the long grass and fired steadily, forcing the Boers to seek shelter in a screen of trees.

Despite the uneven odds, a ferocious gun battle ensued that ended only when the Canadians' ammunition was exhausted, seventeen of their men were either dead or wounded and Carruthers was captured. Although wounded, Perry fought until he died. Wilkinson, who was wounded in the arm (which was eventually amputated) and body, continued firing until he was shot in the eye, then threw the bolt of his rifle into the long grass. Wounded dangerously in six places, Private John A. Minchin followed suit. Private Charles Napier Evans, whose brother was at his side, was no less courageous. Although "mortally wounded through the bowels, he exhausted his ammunition, secured another bandolier, used it up, and as the Boers were making their final rush, he broke his rifle, rendering it useless."[133] Evans died shortly after he was brought into camp. The CMR's commanding officer exaggerated little when he wrote that the "splendid stand by Lieutenant Carruthers' party, without cover of any kind, and against overwhelming odds, was well worthy of the best traditions of Canada and the whole Empire."

The Boer assault on the British lines continued for an hour or so; meanwhile a stranded party of six from Carruthers' troops, under the command of Corporal Knisley — one of the Liliefontein heroes — began a desperate flight for their lives. Cut off from their comrades during the initial onslaught and unable to rejoin their regiment, they decided to make their way back to Klerksdorp. Encouraged by their first day's progress, the men travelled under cover of darkness, stopping only an hour or two to rest and feed their horses their last rations.

Despite their growing hunger and exhaustion, the men continued the next day without difficulty until about 4:00 p.m., when they encountered a party of Boers. Taking shelter in a cornfield, they warded off their pursuers with a few shots. But as soon as they emerged from the cornfield, a larger, more persistent party of Boers appeared and the Canadians took refuge in a native sheep kraal and fought off their assailants until darkness, then made a six-mile detour around the Boer guards in torrential rains until hunger and exhaustion forced them to retire. But they had only bought time.

The next day (2 April) they established defensive positions on a nearby kopje, where they constructed extended stone breastworks, determined to fight to the finish. Within a few hours, eight Boer scouts appeared, followed by a larger force. The Canadians waited until the scouts were within their range. When two of the Boer scouts fell, fifty more Boers joined the battle. The Canadians continued to fire for five hours until their ammunition was exhausted and Corporal Knisley and Private Thomas Bertrand Day were dead. Then the other four called for a ceasefire and surrendered.

The Boers were often generous opponents. Impressed by the Canadians' performance, as soon as they had disarmed the four survivors they congratulated them for their courage and explained in their limited English that they were fighting for their homes. According to one of the Canadian survivors, Private Bert Brace, the Boers knelt with the Canadians as they buried Knisley and Day. Before doing so, the Boers, who had a desperate need for clothing, stripped the dead, leaving Knisley's Distinguished Conduct Medal and his Queen's South Africa ribbon to be buried with his body. Then they stripped the survivors, issued them with a safe conduct and let them continue on their way. Two days and fifty miles later the four starving, exhausted, nearly naked men reached Klerksdorp and were admitted to hospital. When they had recovered from their five-day ordeal, Brace and his comrades returned to place a stone over their dead comrades' graves.

Canadian heroism had exacted a terrible toll. Thirteen Canadians — over half from one Ontario troop — had been killed or would later die of wounds. Among their number was Corporal Alfred A. Sherritt, a twenty-three-year-old, book-keeper from Brantford, son of a Church of England clergyman, a 185-pound athlete who had won the Canadian bicycle championship and had represented Canada at the world competition in Vienna in 1898. Forty other men had been wounded, seven dangerously. Fifty-three of the 164 British casualties were Canadians, the largest Canadian casualty count since Paardeberg. During all this time the 10th Canadian Field Hospital, which had accompanied the column, administered to the wounded in limited shelter, in torrential rains and under fire. Evans subsequently singled out four of its staff for special commendation.

Once the battle ended, each unit buried its dead. The Canadians gathered in the garden of the Boschbult Farm to lay eight of their comrades side by side in a wet common trench, while Evans read the burial service in the pouring rain and a bugler sounded the last post. Eight crosses marked the grave and a rough-hewn gravestone was placed in the centre of the plot upon which one of the Canadians had inscribed with a bayonet and jackknife: "To the Memory Of The Canadian Mounted Rifles Who Fell In Action Here On March 31st 1902." The inscription was surmounted with a maple leaf.

Canadians at home learned of the Harts River battle through a New York news despatch. Thousands of Canadians thronged to bulletin boards to await the details. The next day all major urban newspapers carried elaborations furnished by the British military authorities. Lord Kitchener declared that there "have been few finer instances of heroism in the whole course of the campaign." "Not since Paardeberg," the Toronto *Globe* lamented, "have the wires borne to Canada news so glorious and so mournful." In fact, the subsequent public pride and private sorrow revived "the old time interest in the war." Some claimed that it greatly facilitated recruitment for

Canada's last contingents, the 3rd, 4th, 5th and 6th CMR, units that arrived too late to see active service.

Canadians proudly quoted the long list of British congratulatory cables, from both notables and press reports. They relished the New York *Sun's* invidious comparison between Canadian gallantry and "Australian ruffianness," an allusion to the recent trial and conviction of lieutenants Harry Harbord "Breaker" Morant and Peter Joseph Handcock. When the Minister of Militia, whose son had been killed in an earlier engagement, rose in the Commons to report the sad news of Harts River, members listened in silence as he concluded his remarks with the simple comment that "Canadians are maintaining the reputation that they have already earned in South Africa and they continue to prefer death to surrender."

Carruthers' behaviour received special attention. According to Sir Richard Cartwright, "No soldier in the annals of history has shown greater bravery." Upon his return to Kingston, Carruthers was hailed as a hero and presented with a Sword of Honour. Private citizens such as John A. Ewan committed their feelings to verse. In his thirteen-stanza Kiplingesque poem entitled "Little Hart River," Ewan concluded:

They could die, but they could not surrender,
Could not smirch Canada's name.
And we who survive will remember
Their deed, their death and their fame.

Communities focused on local heroes. In Port Hope, the town's schoolchildren raised money to commission a portrait of Evans, unveiled by the recently knighted Sir Frederick Borden on 31 October 1902. In Cayuga, a life-sized statue of Knisley was erected to commemorate the men from Haldimand County who had served in the war.

The Harts River Battle had caught the public imagination in a way that no other Canadian battle of the South African War had, except Paardeberg. For many years, veterans met for their annual Harts River/Boschbult Banquet, complete with fancy printed menu and entertainment. It was an occasion to affirm their faith in a citizen soldiery and in Canadian military autonomy — sentiments that led many and their followers into and through an even bloodier conflict.[134]

12
SINGING THEIR OWN CANADIAN WAR SONG

In South Africa the graves of Canada's 270 dead are easily identifiable from a distance. Their large granite stones stand out among the simple wooden or iron crosses that mark the remains of other British and colonial soldiers. On the stones 'Canada' is inscribed on the top of their black facing, with a large maple leaf below. These memorials are the work of the Canadian South African Memorial Association, established in February 1902 to identify, mark and care for the graves of Canada's war dead. The memorials speak eloquently of Canada's desire for distinctiveness within the imperial family, a desire that was enhanced by their sons' relations with imperial troops.[135]

The Canadian government had insisted on their troops' distinctiveness in organization, clothing and equipment. But in South Africa, as the loss and the wear and tear of war obliterated these material distinctions, Canadian soldiers became sensitive to the social and cultural distinctions that separated them from their imperial comrades. They noted their differ-

ences of accent and expression, preferences for songs and sports, of attitudes and manners. Strathcona's Horse had gone out of its way to construct a quintessential Canadian image; ironically none was keener to promote this image than some of the British-born recruits! Generally Canadians preferred to serve in Canadian units under Canadian officers. And they had little tolerance for Canadians who aped British mannerisms.

The war sharpened Canadian soldiers' sense of separateness. The British Army's initial difficulty with the Boers' unorthodox methods of warfare challenged Canadians' confidence in British military leadership. Presumptuous British regulars had told Canadians before the war that Canada's poorly trained citizen soldiers could not conceive of fighting effectively with British regulars. But the Canadian troops who had fought at Liliefontein, Harts River and elsewhere and had seen British regulars flee, leaving Canada's citizen soldiers to face overwhelming odds, drew other conclusions from their experience. And when Canadians were reminded that armies required organization and structure, veterans remembered the British Army's chronic failure to provide adequate food and water supplies and their pathetic medical service, dispensed according to rank and title rather than need. Indeed so confident had some Canadian soldiers become of their martial skills that Lieutenant Richard Turner, one of Canada's four Victoria Cross winners, felt that the Canadians had "taught the Regulars how to fight."[136]

Canadians on the home front and warfront drew dubious, heavily Darwinian conclusions from their observations. They attributed some British units' slowness, lethargy and slovenliness to social and physical causes, to 'race' deterioration, urbanization and industrialization and contrasted this with their own country, a classless "land of hope for all who toil," of energetic, independent citizens that could regenerate the Empire and become the future seat of imperial greatness.[137]

Many Canadian officers said that British officers made them and other colonials "feel that they were only members of the mess by sufferance."[138] Conflict between colonial and imperial officers, especially recently promoted junior imperial officers of tenuous social standing, reached such levels that both Roberts and Kitchener issued confidential orders regretting the "unfriendly spirit of regimental officers to members of H.M. colonial forces."[139]

Conflict with imperial troops sharpened Canadian soldiers' sense of distinctiveness. Conflict took various forms, from recreational competitions, verbal sparring and barroom brawls to more serious group confrontations. Some senior officers, like Steele, encouraged rivalry as a means of building morale, establishing borders, defining and reinforcing differences. Some Canadian conflicts attracted public attention; others received little public notice. One incident occurred in December 1901, while the men of Canada's second contingent waited to board a vessel to return to Canada.

Celebrations began soon after the CMR and Dragoons left Pretoria by rail for the Cape. At Kronstad, while their officers enjoyed a champagne dinner, the men commandeered a carload of beer and became disorderly and insubordinate. Things deteriorated considerably at Cape Town, where they were billeted at Maitland Camp with about five hundred Australian troops.

The day after the Canadians reached the Cape, while loading their baggage aboard the *Roslin Castle*, they heard rumours of hijinks in the town but were refused leave to spend their last night in Cape Town. They decided to go nonetheless. Sore "as hell," the Canadians and Australians walked out of camp determined "to have a good time before they sailed."[140]

When officers and sentries tried to stop them, one group hijacked a horse cab. One of the men mounted the horse, another took the reins on the box and the rest crowded in behind. Gathering up speed, the Canadians approached the sentries at a gallop. The Canadians' 'cavalry' charge overcame the British guards and they were "obliged to make way for the cab and its load."[141] The men headed straight for the bars on Adderly Street.

Some of the Canadians had just entered their first bar when a military order arrived to sell no drinks to anyone. When the hotel management's attempts to explain the order failed, the thirsty men took matters into their own hands. The bar was "shot up in wild western fashion. Pistol bullets shattered the chandeliers. Men tried to shoot their monograms into the big plate glass mirror… others vaulted the bar and worked as volunteer barmen." They then visited the Grand Hotel where the manager informed them of his inability to sell liquor. But nothing prevented him from giving it away, he said, so long as they left the bar intact. The men accepted his hospitality, respected his request and collected three Canadian hats full of gold sovereigns as a gratuity. As news of the Grand's largesse spread, a crowd of thirsty customers packed the hotel and two city blocks. "Traffic was stopped. The military police saw they couldn't do a thing with the mob, so they did not try."[142]

This was not just a Canadian riot. The Australians were on their way home and had a score to settle with a "Dutch paper" that had called them "descendants of convicts." The Australians visited their accusers, "wrecked the plant and were now marching about the town looking for trouble in general." Incapable of containing the situation, the city police called upon the military authorities. About thirty Cape Mounted Rifles "supported by infantry patrols with fixed bayonets formed in line and drew their swords, then chose the most solid looking body of rioters, and advanced at a walk, broke into a trot and finally a gallop. They used the flats and the backs of their swords and cracked many heads."[143] The mob broke up and the men found their way back to camp, carrying their casualties of sword and the bar.

The British military authorities' response was strikingly indulgent. They initiated no extensive investigation, and made no efforts to single out and punish the offenders and their leaders. Men who were 'absent without leave' received a mere seven days' detention, a meaningless sentence, given the number of men and the fact that they were aboard ship. There is also a reference in Captain Turner's diary that they "paid for their spree like real men,"

perhaps by a voluntary fine or a collection to cover the property damages. Turner's lighthearted reference suggests that the British military authorities had dismissed the riot as youthful high spirits; and since they were colonial citizen soldiers it would have been unwise to pursue them.

The riot did nothing to quell the cordiality of the official departure ceremonies for the Canadian and Australian troops the next day. The British High Commissioner, the British military authorities and the Cape Town Mayor thanked and praised the colonial troops for their service. The Mayor even promised an unspecified souvenir for each soldier, something that could be passed down with pride to his or her family for generations. The city's spectators were no less warm in their reception of the previous evening's happy rioters as they marched peacefully through their streets to the awaiting vessels — perhaps relieved to see them depart!

Occasionally conflict reached dangerous levels of misun-

Commemorative items

derstanding. The most spectacular example featured two troops of Canadian constables in Baden-Powell's South African Constabulary. Social tensions compounded misunderstandings, since few of the Canadian constables came from the social class that Baden-Powell had hoped to recruit from "all over the Empire": experienced, well-bred, skilled horsemen and land-hungry settlers, which he procured with little difficulty among the sons of the British gentry. Although many of the Canadian con-

stables were South African veterans, others were urban shop hands and drifters. Many were adventurers — wild, reckless and rowdy men, who had joined the unit in the dead of winter and were anxious to participate in the fighting. Few had any real interest in settling into the more sedate, sedentary life of a constable in a quiet African town, much less becoming a farmer.

Baden-Powell recognized the social difference at once. While he realized that the Canadian constables were hard-working and "brave to foolhardy in the field,"[144] an observation reinforced by their casualties, he regretted their resistance to sedentary, blockhouse consignments.

Although tensions between Canadian and British authorities smouldered during the war, once hostilities ceased and the constables were consigned to isolated, sedentary civilian employment, a serious crisis developed, precipitated by the need to reduce the force. The cost-conscious War Office ordered a reduction of the force by 40%, an irresistible invitation to the police authorities to "weed out the rotters." In reconstructing his peacetime force, Baden-Powell wanted only the steady, able, educated men who would give no offence to the Boer population so "easily offended by the slightest impropriety in language and demeanour."[145] During his purge, Canadians felt that they had been targeted as victims of systematic discrimination, deception and the "spiteful and petty tyranny of imperial officers," and they reacted strongly.[146]

The conflict came to a head during the summer of 1903, in Troops 14 and 17,

Awards and medals

units composed of men from Saint John, New Brunswick and Montreal. After a rigorous tour of inspection, a supercilious imperial career officer, recently recruited from the ranks, reported that these troops' interior economy was disastrous. Discipline was lax and men displayed no deference to rank and seniority. Many were insubordinate, ignorant of rules and regulations, lacking in initiative and "mutinous, dishonest and drunken." Upon receipt of this devastating report, the Divisional Commander reprimanded the Canadian captains commanding these troops and ordered them to restore order at once. When the captains failed to comply, they were informed that they were to be replaced by imperial officers.

The troops' response was immediate and "mutinous." The men petitioned their Divisional Commander, denouncing the proposed transfer, and threatening to serve only under Canadian officers who "understand the Canadian disposition." When their petition failed, the troops' non-commissioned officers demanded permission to revert to the ranks. When their threat was ignored, the Canadians raised the stakes. On the day of the transfer, the Canadian constables left their posts without orders and went into town leaving "the district without police," obliging the sub-divisional commander to replace them temporarily with police from other districts.

The sub-divisional commander arrested the 'strike' leaders. Nine men went on trial in Bloemfontein, but a board of offi-cers failed to extract evidence from the tightly-knit group, none willing to implicate the other. In the end it was impossible to establish individual guilt and lay charges. Nonetheless, they and twenty-four others were discharged, most with no entry on their defaulters sheet, and some whose conduct was described as "very good."

About one hundred Canadian constables returned to Canada claiming they had been victims of national discrimination; alto-gether some 720 of Canada's 1,200 constables left the service before the expiry of their service. Their complaints received a sympathetic public hearing. "Canadians are not, nor does the public opinion of this country demand that Canadians become the lackeys of English officers," wrote one irate correspondent. "A Canadian trooper is a fighting man; he is not a soldier."[147] During a House of Commons debate on the issue, Sir Frederick Borden requested that the British authorities open an investigation, which subsequently and predictably cleared the imperial officers of all blame. Many of the Canadians' allegations, however, were well-founded — though motivated less by national prejudice than by the Constabulary's careless, chaotic, incompetent and often petty administration. Public discussion of this issue reinforced Canadians' view of imperial officers and the society they were thought to represent.

Imperial authorities often encouraged national difference. They appreciated the role of local identities in building regimental loyalties and *esprit de corps*. In their greetings and communications with Canadian troops and in language and music, senior British officers invited Canadian troops to articulate a national persona within the imperial family. For example, Baden-Powell made 'Canada' the password the first night after the celebrated relief of Mafeking, to recognize the contribution of the Royal Canadian Field Artillery.

Other senior officers went out of their way to meet, greet and thank Canadian troops. During farewell ceremonies and

Visiting war graves in South Africa

on other occasions, British officers invited Canadians to sing Canadian songs such as "The Land of the Maple Is the Land for Me" and British bands flattered Canadians with Canadian tunes such as "Vive la Canadienne" or the "Maple Leaf Forever," or employed other appropriate alternatives such as "Cock of the North." Moreover, close association with the Gordon Highlanders and other British regular units with strong regional and regimental identities invited emulation.

Popular British writers, such as Richard Jebb, Rudyard Kipling and Arthur Conan Doyle supplied language, argument and imagery to articulate the colonial difference. In speeches, reports and stories they cast colonial troops as youthful, courageous, resourceful, unorthodox and energetic, images that Canadian commanders exploited to their advantage. The Elgin Commission of 1903 described Canadian and colonial troops as "half soldier by their upbringing, natural horsemen, observant scouts, whose officers share with their men mutual interests, and whose men are trained to think for themselves, and…carry on should their leaders be killed." The British *Lancet* described Boers and colonials as physically larger, stronger, and fitter than the British Tommy, and "man for man…incomparably superior to our workers in London or Manchester or Glasgow."[148] This was heady stuff!

Although Canada's soldiers' conflicts with imperial authorities scarcely enhanced their image as ambassadors of the 'peaceable kingdom,' their association with imperial troops gave them a sense of their own distinctiveness. Many who left Canada as 'sons of the Empire,' returned "Singing Their Own Canadian War Song," a refrain echoed by civilians at home.

13

CANADA'S WAR

Remembering is at the "heart of national identity."[149] Commemorative place names, statues, memorials, books, photographs, songs, poems, prints and drawings construct and reinforce a collective memory.

They memorialize dates, deeds and persons. They celebrate allegiance and values; they invite emulation and example.

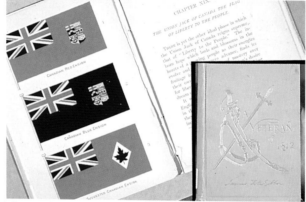

The Maple Leaf and the Union Jack

Together they create a sense of shared experience, community and belonging, sometimes at variance with contemporary realities. The memory of Canada's Boer War has bequeathed a mixed, ambiguous legacy, one that fuelled the cause of nation building, though not always the same nation.

Canada's Boer War was more than a distraction. Altogether Canada recruited some 7,368 men for the war — many veterans of previous contingents. At least 349 of these recruits demobilized in South Africa, where some found lucrative civilian employment. Others joined British irregular units such as Kitchener's Scouts, Roberts' Horse, Brabant's

Horse or Howard's Canadian Scouts. A cursory examination of 714 attestation papers of British irregulars found 167 men with some previous Canadian connection. Moreover, a large number of Canadian graduates of the Royal Military College in the British Army served in the South African War. The best known was Lieutenant-Colonel Percy Girouard, the famous French Canadian railway engineer who rose to great prominence in the British Army. Civilians, too, served in a variety of non-combatant support roles: chaplains, doctors, nurses, dentists, postmen, teachers, blacksmiths, artisans and peacemakers.

A striking example of civilian engagement was the recruitment toward the end of the war of twenty-four female teachers. They were part of Milner's final solution, his so-called 'civilizing' mission, the pacification of South Africa, of which the South African Constabulary was one instalment. In Milner's larger plan, education played a central role: to teach Afrikaners the English language and civic values. To achieve this objective, he sought single, female teachers, educational missionaries willing to live and work in small towns, villages and rural areas — and provide wives to settlers, preferably his Constables. The Canadian government found no dearth of well-educated, adventuresome candidates.

Indeed they had many more than they needed to fill the twenty-four Canadian places assigned to this imperial project.

Nevertheless, one can exaggerate the relative importance of Canada's contribution. After all, the number of Canadian citizen soldiers was roughly equal to New Zealand's contribution, a country with a fraction of Canada's population, and a stark contrast to Australia's sixteen thousand men.[149]

Canada's contribution is even more modest when one realizes that two thousand of its 7,368 men, those of the 3rd, 4th, 5th and 6th CMR, arrived too late to see active service. Nor did the Canadian government or public demonstrate much enthusiasm for the recruitment of these final contingents. Laurier himself thought the British request "injudicious," given the public's hostility toward their recruitment.

Moreover, it is easy to forget Canada's continuing ambiguity to the war, best exemplified by a curious initiative to have Canada's Prime Minister serve as a mediator between Boer and Briton, oblivious to the fact that Canada was a belligerent.

In December 1900 a *Times* report from Ottawa suggested that Laurier be asked to broker a peace settlement. The suggestion triggered a lively debate in the British and Canadian press. While most Canadian papers favoured the proposal, British papers disagreed, except the *Daily Mail* and the *Manchester Guardian*. The *Manchester Guardian*'s Harold Spender was the proposal's most eloquent advocate. Spender believed that Laurier, coming from a linguistic minority, would "be able to bring some of this Canadian healing to bear on the gaping wounds of South Africa."[150]

Canada's most ardent advocate was W.D. "Shuyler" Lighthall (in communications on this topic he insisted on his middle name), a bilingual Montreal novelist, poet, lawyer and local politician, of self-described "old Dutch stock." Before the war, Lighthall, who introduced himself to his Boer audience as "an intensely friendly spectator," corresponded with Jan Hendrick Hofmeyer, the influential leader of the Afrikaner Bond and an MP for Stellenbosch, whom Lighthall considered "a moderate peace loving and able man," on how one might resolve the South African crisis short of war. At the time, Hofmeyer was attempting to mediate between Milner and Kruger.

In May 1899, Hofmeyer published Lighthall's "appeal to his 'Boer cousins' for a reasoned settlement" in the South African *Telegraph*. In his address, Lighthall appealed to progressive, 'moderate' Boers, those opposed to Kruger's politics, citing Canada as an example of linguistic and cultural harmony within the Empire. Lighthall's appeal for mediation resembled Kruger's final call for international arbitration.

Failure to resolve differences short of war continued to trouble Lighthall. Convinced that Hofmeyer was now "the most able man in South Africa," in early January 1901, Lighthall wrote him in Munich, suggesting that Laurier be asked to mediate the outstanding issues and end the war of attrition.[151] His purpose was "to lift affairs permanently out of the sphere of bloodshed back to its proper sphere of diplomacy."[152] While he realized that the British had refused arbitration outside the Empire, he was confident that they might consider mediation from within. And he was persuaded that Laurier had the credentials to negotiate a settlement, and that Canada provided a model for the coexistence of Boer and Britain within South Africa.

When Hofmeyer responded positively, Lighthall immediately consulted F.L. Beique, a close friend of Laurier. At first somewhat wary, Laurier agreed to serve if the Boers requested his mediation and the British consented — both highly unlikely conditions.[153] In the end, Laurier's conditions could not be secured, and the correspondence appears to have ended. Nevertheless, the idea of Laurier as a mediator and Canada as a relevant example for South Africa died a slow death. As late as April 1902, John Charlton and Henri Bourassa, Liberals who disagreed strongly on the

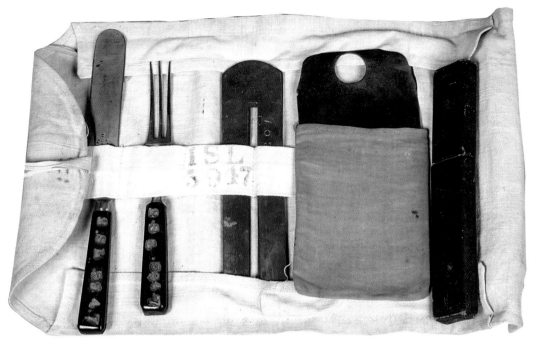

Mess kit

for various causes.

Boer War heroes and battles continued to fascinate and entertain. Perhaps none was more visible than Baden-Powell and his Boy Scout movement and its war-inspired uniforms and philosophy. On a more popular level, in 1904 Frank Fallis even staged a re-enactment of the Battle of Paardeberg at the Louisiana Purchase Worlds Fair in St. Louis,

war, introduced a House of Commons motion calling for "the broadest policy of magnanimity and mercy" toward the Boers in negotiating a peace, a motion that failed to come to a vote.[154]

Lighthall continued to preach fraternity and build bridges. Three days before the war's end he published a four-page pamphlet entitled "To The Boers A Friend's Appeal From Canada," lauding the Boer military commanders' bravery, condemning their bad political leaders and calling for the unification of the country along the lines pioneered by Canada.[155] His admiration and sympathy for the Boers was not singular, even during the war,[156] and underscores Canada's continued ambiguity toward the war.

Nevertheless commentators and activists mined the Boer War for meaning and morals. Military thinkers and reformers sought lessons to support changes in strategy, tactics, organization and *matériel*. Social reformers cited British military weaknesses to promote and implement social programs designed to 'regenerate' the British people and create a strong and healthy 'race' capable of confronting the next conflict. Novelists romanticized the conflict and used it to proselytize

featuring Cronje and some 250 of his warriors. Although his compatriots and their wartime supporters denounced his, "benefiting from the sorrow of his people," the display attracted thousands of spectators, a testament to the war's fascination and led to its enactment elsewhere.

The war seems to have left little rancour between Canada and South Africa. The yellow press's characterization of the Boers as cruel, ignorant, fanatical peasants corresponded little with the Canadian soldiers' experience. Boer soldiers, of course, came in various guises and their unorthodox tactics sometimes entailed deception and treachery; these acts elicited anger and calls for vengeance. Incidents in the Steelpoort Valley, for example, made their commandos particularly unpopular with the Royal Canadian Dragoons.

Generally, however, Canadian soldiers came to admire the Boers as warriors and learned from their tactics. Post-war Canadian military reorganization owes much to their experiences in this conflict. Canadian war prisoners were well-treated. When they were wounded they received care and consideration; and the remains of Canadians killed in battle were treated with respect and occasionally with admiration.

One member of the Royal Canadians who became a temporary prisoner of General De Wet at Roodeval wrote: "I would like to record here and now the fact that they could not have treated us as prisoners of war in a better way. Shared all their food, issued a wool white blanket…"[157] Consequently when a Boer farm delegation, containing a number of prominent Boer leaders, toured Canada almost immediately after the war, they were received warmly and enthusiastically wherever they went.

For many Canadians the war had a special claim on their public and private memory. Some saw it from the beginning as "Our War," to quote Winnipeg's Wesley College Student's journal *Vox*.[158] Others viewed it as a natural extension of Canada's experience and history, its struggle for "liberty and civilization." T.G. Marquis, the professor of English at Queen's University, prolific author and strident war advocate, compared the Uitlanders to the Canadian reformers and their struggle for responsible government, or the Canada party's role in the Red River resistance. He and others likened the South African

Canadian scout uniform inspired by the war

Chartered Company to the Hudson's Bay Company and its 'civilizing' mission to the Canadian prairie. Others compared it to their Militia's repulsion of the American invasions of 1775, 1812 and later the Fenian raiders. In this context it was indeed 'Our War,' our citizen soldiers defending another corner of the imperial estate.

The war empowered many English Canadians, gave them "a sense of power," to use Carl Berger's characterization of Canadian imperialism. In their memorials, patriotic lectures, stories and sermons about the war, Canadians constructed a national mythology informed by the war. Whatever their internal divisions, some of the Canadian contingents invented, cultivated and projected a collective persona designed to set them apart within the imperial family.

The civilian population echoed these refrains and applied them to civic society. They emphasized British military incompetence and failure, the common British soldiers' inferior physical condition, their mindless deference to class and social distinctions, in contrast to their own energy, initiative, resourcefulness, independence and freedom from constraint. This self-confidence fed a claim for greater self-reliance and autonomy, and an enhanced leadership role within the Empire.

Canada's first overseas military expedition provided Canada's nascent Militia with history, tradition, insignia and an autonomist agenda. Strathcona's Horse and the Canadian Mounted Rifles owe their creation to the war. The Royal Canadian Dragoons' regimental insignia, a springbok on a scroll, and Strathcona's Horse's regimental march, "Soldiers of the Queen," give the war a pride of place in their regimental traditions. Militia units that contributed men to the Canadian contingents proudly trooped battle honours earned in South African engagements.

Perhaps no insignia stimulated greater pride than the maple leaf 'Canada' badge affixed to the men's helmets or service caps, on either side of their collars or on both of their shoulder straps. During the war, the maple leaf served various purposes: to locate campgrounds, celebrate a fortification, identify the group, or mark the final resting place of a fallen comrade. Some men first learned the words and music of "The Land of the Maple" and the "Maple Leaf Forever" in South Africa; for many the latter became something of a national anthem. Others explained their motive for recruitment in emblematic terms: they had enlisted to "hold up the Maple Leaf Forever," and consoled themselves that if they died "t'will help the Maple Leaf to Live."[159]

The war created Canadian military heroes: Harold Borden, William Knisley, Bruce Carruthers, Edward Holland (after whom Holland Barracks in Ottawa was named), R.E.W. Turner and others. The battles at Paardeberg, Liliefontein and Harts River called for annual commemoration. Boer War organizations such as the Boer War Veterans Association, the South African Veterans Mutual Protection Association, the Patriotic Fund, the Canadian Soldiers' Wives League, the Imperial Order of the Daughters of the Empire and the South African Memorial Association institutionalized the war's memory. As veterans gathered for their annual Paardeberg, Liliefontein or Harts River Day celebrations, memories of their failures, their interpersonal strife and conflict, death, disease and discouragement were displaced by more heroic versions of the war and how it was won. Veterans

and their audience soon came to believe their own rhetoric.

No tale became imbued with greater patriotic significance than the Battle of Paardeberg. "Today, Canada is a nation," wrote one proud war chronicler.[160] Civilians were especially fanciful in imagining the battle's lesson. It began with Laurier's reference to Paardeberg as a coming of age: "a bold declaration that a new power had arisen in the West."[161] Similarly, another commentator explained that Canadians had not rejoiced because Cronje was defeated, but because their sons had become men in the eyes of the world."[162] To another, it demonstrated clearly "what nation was going to rule the world." The hero of Jeanette Duncan's 1904 novel *The Imperialist* captured this 'sense of power' in his rhetorical question: "In the scrolls of the future is it not written that the centre of the Empire must shift — and where, if not to Canada?"[163] In other words, the war had demonstrated that Canada was no longer a dependent but an imperial partner, if not the future nerve centre of a regenerated Empire.

Canada's war-engendered confidence sought greater autonomy. Veterans of Liliefontein, Harts River and other engagements, who had watched in dismay as British Regulars fled, leaving Canadians to fend for themselves, were determined that in the next war Canadian troops would form one division and that Canadian officers would command Canadian troops. At home they insisted that Canadian Militia officers command their own Militia, and that their defence policy and Militia organization reflect their needs and assumptions.

They were equally insistent that Canada possess distinctive kit and equipment, including the notorious Ross Rifle with which they entered World War I. In the years following the war, the Minister of Militia, backed by the House of Commons' militia lobby, cited the lessons of war to justify reform of the militia. He abolished the office of GOC, which had been reserved for British regular officers, promoted Canadian officers to senior militia positions, increased the military estimates, enlarged its establishment, raised its pay scales, re-equipped it with new rifles and artillery and purchased a large central training base at Petawawa. He introduced higher standards of training and promotion and more serviceable uniforms. He used the war as an opportunity to test tents, transport ambulance wagons, water carts, hospital equipment and supplies — some of Canadian design. After the war, he established an Army Service Corps, a Corps of Signals, a Corps of Guides, an Ordnance Corps, a Veterinary Corps and a Pay Corps.

The war also affected military policy and planning. It gave credence to proponents of the militia myth, those who preferred a trained citizenry to a professional, standing army, a preference that shaped the direction of post-war military reform and reorganization. Borden's decision to establish a decentralized, citizen army of sharpshooters, his attempt to secure a dependable Canadian supply of rifles and ammunition, his subsidization of rifle clubs and his encouragement of cadet corps, military training in the schools and later Baden-Powell's Boy Scouts, were all inspired by the 'lessons' of the Boer War. So too was Borden's insistence upon Canadian military autonomy and pragmatic, cooperative imperialism rather than imperial integration, all policies that enjoyed wide popular support.

Canadian claims for greater autonomy exceeded defence policy. Indeed the first call for the creation of a Canadian Department of External Affairs was published in Sanford Evans, *The Canadian Contingents and Canadian Imperialism: A Story and a Study (1901)*.

Numerous public monuments to the Boer War — often large, impressive structures in central urban spaces — testify to Canadians' desire to remember their role in this conflict. During and following the war, the organization, funding and inauguration of an impressive number of monuments provided an occasion to construct and propagate patriotic lessons. Confident of the didactic value of public monuments, in the decade following the Boer War, the erection of memorial windows, plaques, busts, statues and cenotaphs in schools, universities, churches, armouries and other public places became something of a minor industry. Some memorials were dedicated to individual heroes such as Borden, Knisley, Carruthers, Holland and Turner. Most monuments honoured collective service and lauded loyalty, patriotism, duty, courage

Spoils of war

and sacrifice. Many public monuments were erected by individuals or civic, corporate and patriotic bodies, at considerable cost.

The war's popularity had solid economic foundations. The demand for military boots, clothing, saddlery, food, forage and horses fuelled Canada's manufacturing, agriculture, transportation and service industries. Many farmers, manufacturers, retailers, shippers, bankers, insurance brokers and advertisers enjoyed a lively war business. Request for military goods came from the British government as well. Altogether, the British War Office purchased seven and a half million dollars worth of Canadian goods during the war, including horses and forage.

Conscious of the opportunities for expanding trade with South Africa during wartime and post war reconstruction, the Canadian government sent an agent to South Africa to develop Canadian trade. There he met Canadian representatives of entrepreneurs already at work for the Massey Harris Company, the Canadian Carriage Company and the Dominion Radiator Company. Determined to facilitate trade, the Canadian government subsidized a direct steamship service to South Africa.

Private interests seized the opportunity. The Canadian Manufacturers Association's journal, *Industrial Canada*, vigorously promoted Canadian trade with South Africa, boasting that Canadian troops in South Africa were excellent advertisements, and providing advice on trade tactics and strategies. Industrial and agricultural exhibitions in Canada and abroad used Canada's war contribution to promote trade. The cover for the Canadian catalogue for the Glasgow Exhibition of August 1901 displayed two Canadians in khaki, with the Canadian coat of arms on the back. At home, the Central Canada Exhibition in July 1900 depicted Cronje's surrender at Paardeberg. Trade calendars and Christmas cards with military scenes underscored a company's patriotic credentials. "Those who fell were hardly cold," W. Sanford Evans complained in the *Canadian Magazine*, "before they were stripped by those who would build metaphorical foundations of empire with their bones: and others so far forgot themselves as to dilate upon the value of such things as national advertisement, being sure that henceforth our immigration literature would be in greater demand and our food products more popular. They were willing to make a blood-and-bones poster out of our heroes."[164]

The growing popularity of Empire in the last quarter of the nineteenth century however posed a challenge to settlement colonies of mixed ethnic and linguistic heritage. Nowhere was this more evident than in South Africa and in Canada. Efforts to define and reorder the imperial estate around shared trade, defence and political objectives confronted colonial vested interests and threatened to upset the liberal constitutional settlement based on local autonomy and responsible government. Even less successful were attempts to create a cultural community around language, race and religion. The outbreak of war in South Africa in October 1899 tested the limits of this discourse in a bilingual and bi-ethnic country such as Canada.

Nonetheless the post-war historical construction of French Canada's reaction to the war is often at variance with the record. For example, Laurier's prediction that the war would unite Canadians across linguistic fault lines was less fanciful at the time than it became after World War I. Although initially no French Canadian journal advocated Canadian participation in the war, once the government decided to dispatch troops large dailies such as *Le Journal, La Presse, Le Soleil* and *La Patrie* accepted even if they did not support the war.[165] After Black Week, others such as Jules-Paul Tardivel's *La Verite* worried about the possibility of British defeat and its effect upon Canadian safety on this continent. Whatever their sympathies, French Canadians appeared to have remained "passively loyal," like their English Canadian compatriots

The twentieth century belongs to Canada

"content to be a protected colony."[166]

The Boer War, however, became an unfortunate historical reference point, especially after the Conscription Crisis of 1917. Although French Canadian opposition to participation had dissipated, especially after Black Week, resentments remained acute among nationalists, resentments that increasingly coalesced around Henri Bourassa and a growing number of other political disputes and causes. A charismatic young Liberal MP, Bourassa had resigned his seat in the House of Commons to protest Canada's participation in the war, then successfully re-contested the seat. In the House of Commons he remained a trenchant critic of Canada's participation and the British conduct of the war.

Moreover, during the war French Canadians had voted with their feet; only 3% of the Canadian volunteers were French Canadians — though they were better represented among officers, who they served with distinction. Finally the Montreal riot served as a stern reminder of the war's mixed legacy.

The war gave some Canadians a new sense of cohesion, power, importance, confidence, self-reliance and place in the community of nations — and provided identity and definition. To others, it became a bitter reference point, a legacy of disillusionment and deception. To those more sensitive to the limitations of imperialism in a bi-national country, it served as a wake-up call, a stern warning to pragmatic politicians toying with schemes for imperial reorganization. The war, then, left a divided heritage, one that an embarrassed post–World War I generation of historians attempted to explain, excuse and blame on a group of imperial conspirators.

NOTES

[1] This figure is the aggregate of the strength of all units recruited in Canada, and is somewhat misleading, given the large number of men who served in more than one Canadian unit.

[2] See, Douglas Oscar Skelton, *Life and Letters of Sir Wilfrid Laurier*, two volumes, (Toronto, 1921); Laurent Olivar David, *Laurier: Sa Vie, Ses Oeuvres*, (Beauceville, 1919); John W. Dafoe, *Laurier A Study In Politics* (Toronto, 1922).

[3] H. Pearson Gundy, "Sir Wilfrid Laurier and Lord Minto," Canadian Historical Association Report, 1952.

[4] Carl Berger, *The Sense of Power*, (Toronto, 1970).

[5] Carman Miller, *Painting the Map Red: Canada and the South African War, 1899-1902*, (Montreal, 1993), 104.

[6] Fransjohan Pretorius, *Life On Commando During the Anglo-Boer War, 1899-1902*, (Human and Rousseau, Cape Town), 15.

[7] Jonathan Lewis, "Introduction" in Tabitha Jackson, *The Boer War*, (Channel Four Books, London, 1999), 7.

[8] Laurier L. LaPierre, "Politics, Race and Religion in French Canada: Joseph Israel Tarte," (unpublished Ph.D. thesis, University of Toronto, 1962), 373.

[9] *Hamilton Spectator*, 13 October, 1899.

[10] The *Toronto Mail*, 4 November, 1899; the *Fredericton Reporter*, 27 September, 1899; *The Toronto Evening News*, 11 March, 1899.

[11] Montreal *Star*, 12 October, 1899.

[12] The *Toronto Globe*, 20 October, 1899.

[13] See Carl Berger, *The Sense of Power*, (Toronto, 1969).

[14] *Les Debats*, 10 decembre, 1899.

[15] *Le Temps*, 12 octobre, 1899.

[16] W. Sanford Evans, *The Canadian Contingents*, (Toronto, 1902), 17.

[17] New York Public Library, W. Bourke Cochran Papers, Goldwin Smith to Cochran, 10 November, 1899. I owe this reference to Dr. Edward P. Kohn.

[18] *The Canadian Gleaner*, 12 October, 1899; *Regina Standard*, 25 October, 1899.

[19] National Archives of Canada, hereafter NAC, the R.E.W. Turner Papers, Diary, 26 December, 1900.

[20] *New Denver Ledger*, 2 November, 1899, and 19 October, 1899; *Sandon Paystreak*, 21 October, 1899.

[21] *Citizen and Country*, 4 November, 1899; *Sandon Paystreak*, 14 December, 1899.

[22] *New Denver Ledger*, 20 October, 1899.

[23] *Sandon Paystreak*, 11 November, 1899.

[24] *Citizen and Country*, 9 December, 1899.

[25] Carman Miller, "English-Canadian Opposition to the South African War as seen through the Press," *Canadian Historical Review*, Vol. LV, No 4, December, 1974.

[26] Barry Moody, "Boers and Baptists: Maritime Canadians View the South African War," (unpublished paper presented to the conference on "Canada and the Boer War" held at the Institute for Commonwealth Studies, London, 3-4 March 2000).

[27] *Canadian Churchman*, 12 and 29 October, 1899.

[28] *Canadian Congregationalist*, 12 and 19 October and 2 November, 1899.

[29] Norman Penlington, *Canada and Imperialism 1896-1899*, (Toronto, 1965), 240-241.

[30] E.B Biggar, *The Boer War, Its Causes and Its Interests to Canadians*, (Toronto, 1900), 30-31.

[31] Jean-Guy Pelletier, "La Presse Canadienne-Française et la Guerre des Boers," *Recherches Sociographiques*, Vol. IV, No 3 decembre, 1963.

[32] NAC, J. W. Willison Papers, Laurier to Willison, 5 October, 1899.

[33] *The Bobcaygeon Independent*, 14 October, 1899.

[34] John Willison, *Reminiscences Political and Personal*, (Toronto, 1919), 303-304.

[35] Montreal *Star*, 30 October, 1899.

[36] NAC, Laurier Papers, "Memorandum of the Privy Council Decision," 13 October, 1899.

[37] Montreal *Star*, 14 October, 1899.

[38] Gaston Labat, *Le Livre d'Or*, (Montreal, 1901), 135

[39] Miller, *Painting The Map Red*, 58.

[40] Carman Miller "A Preliminary Analysis of the Socio-economic Composition of Canada's South African War Contingents," *Histoire sociale-Social History* , Vol. VIII, No 16, November, 1975, 219-237.

[41] For a more detailed description of each of the nine units recruited in Canada, see above or Miller, *Painting the Map Red*.

[42] NAC, Walter Bapty Papers, Memoirs, 16.

[43] NAC, Edwin McCormack Papers, Memoirs, 43.

[44] Carman Miller, "Chums in Arms: Comradeship in Canada's South African War Contingents," *Histoire sociale-Social History*, 1986.

[45] Public Record Office, hereafter PRO, Colonial Office 526, Vol. III South African Constabulary, M.O. McCarthy to Assistant Division Staff Officer, 26 June, 1903.

[46] NAC, Mrs Charles Bennett Papers, Arthur Bennett to Mother, 30 December, 1899.

[47] See Annie Mellish, *Our Boys Under Fire*, (Charlottetown, 1900).

[48] Labat, *Le Livre d'Or*, 115-116.

[49] Rosa Shaw, *Proud Heritage*, (Toronto, 1957), 153; Castell Hopkins, ed., *Morang's Annual Register for 1901*, (Toronto, 1901), 308.

[50] Gordon Heath, "Sin in the Camp: The Day of Humble Supplication," *Journal of the Canadian Church Historical Society* , Vol. XLIV 2002.

[51] W. Hart McHarq, *From Quebec to Pretoria with the Royal Canadian Regiment*, (Toronto, 1902), 196.

[52] McHarq, *From Quebec to Pretoria*, 55. Private Collection, Valle Family Papers, Lucien Valle à Papa; 10 avril, 1900.

[53] McHarq, *From Quebec to Pretoria*, 53.

[54] NAC, John Albert Perkins Papers, Albert to Mother, 25 November, 1899.

[55] Julian Ralph, quoted in T.G. Marquis, *Canada's Sons on Kopje and Veldt*, (Toronto, 1900), 117.

[56] NAC, William Otter Papers, Otter to Hubert Foster, 21 January, 1900.

[57] NAC, Mrs Charles Bennett Papers, Arthur Bennett to Mother, 30 December, 1899.

[58] NAC, Albert Perkins Papers, Albert to Mother, 2 January, 1900.

[59] Canada, Sessional Paper 35a (1901), Appendix A1, 43.

[60] NAC, Mrs Charles Bennett Papers, Arthur to Mother, 16 March, 1900.

[61] Labat, *Le Livre d'Or*, 128 and 135.

[62] NAC, F.H Dunham Papers, "Paardeberg", ms, 3.

[63] C. Russell Hubly, *G Company*, Montreal, 1901, 73.

[64] NAC, Otter Papers, Otter to Molly, 25 February, 1900.

[65] T. G. Marquis, *Canada's Sons on Kopje and Veldt*, (Toronto, 1900), 250.

[66] Labat, *Le Livre d'Or*, 146; see also NAC Otter Papers, Otter to Molly, 4 March, 1900.

[67] Christiaan De Wet, *Three Years' War*, (Westminster, 1901), 56 and 63.

[68] Creswicke, South Africa, IV, 78.

[69] Norman Patterson, "The War and Canada," *Canadian Magazine*, July,1902, 204.

[70] NAC Otter Papers, Otter to Molly, 4 March, 1900.

[71] The Montreal *Star*, 11 May, 1900.

[72] I owe this information to the kindness of Craig Wilcox.

[73] Desmond Morton, *The Canadian General, Sir William Otter*, (Toronto, 1974), 202 ff.

[74] For a full account of the riot, see Carman Miller, "The Montreal Flag Riot of 1900," in *One Flag, One Queen, One Tongue*, John Crawford and Ian McGibbon (eds.), (The University of Auckland Press, 2003).

[75] Rumilly, *Histoire de la Province de Québec*, Vol. IX, Montreal, n.d., 174

[76] *The McGill Outlook*, 8 March, 1900.

[77] The *McGill Outlook*, 10 March, 1900.

[78] Tarte to Bruchési, 2 March, 1900, cited in Rumilly, *Histoire de la Province de Québec*, Vol. IX, 178.

[79] *La Patrie*, 2 mars, 1900.

[80] NAC, Minto Papers, Minto to Lansdowne, 2 March, 1900.

[81] Public Record Office, Colonial Office, 42, 875, 7194, Minto to Joseph Chamberlain, 4 March, 1900.

[82] NAC, Minto Papers, Minto to Laurier, 2 March, 1900

[83] NAC, Minto Papers, Minto to William Peterson, 7 March, 1900.

[84]Rumilly, *Histoire de la Province de Québec*, Vol. IX, 179.

[85] McGill University Archives, William Peterson Papers, Préfontaine to Peterson, 2 March, 1900.

[86] *The Citizen and Country*, 11 March 1900

[87] The Montreal *Star*, 3 March, 1900.

[88] NAC, Wilfrid Laurier Papers, Fred H. MacKay to Laurier, 6 March, 1900.

[89] Rumilly, *Histoire de la Province de Québec,* Vol. IX, 174.

[90] *La Patrie*, 2 and 3 mars, 1900.

[91] *The McGill Outlook*, 7 March, 1900, 215.

[92] *Ibid.*, 182.

[93] *Monetary Times*, 9 March, 1900.

[94] *Toronto Globe*, 5 March, 1900.

[95] *Ottawa Citizen*, 5 March, 1900.

[96] *St. James Gazette*, 7 March, 1900.

[97] *St James' Gazette*, 7 March, 1900.

[98] *La Patrie*, 3 mars, 1900.

[99] *La Patrie*, 3 mars, 1900.

[100] *The McGill Outlook*, 19 March, 1900, 226.

[101] NAC, Minto Papers, Minto to Joseph Chamberlain, 24 November, 1900.

[102] *La Presse*, 19 âout, 1933; *Le Petit Journal*, 21 mars, 1948.

[103] G. Russell Hubly, *G Company*, Montreal, 1901, 86.

[104] NAC, Otter Papers, Barker to Otter, 20 March, 1900.

[105] NAC, J.W. Jeffrey Papers, Jeffrey to John, 17 April, 1900.

[106] Emily Hobhouse, *The Brunt of the War and Where it Fell*, (London, 1902); B. Roberts, *Those Bloody Women: Three Heroines of the Boer War*, (London, 1991).

[107] S.B. Spies, *Methods of Barbarism?: Roberts and Kitchener and Civilians in the Boer Republics*, (Cape Town, 1977).

[108] Canada, Sessional Paper 35a (1901), Report A, 28-9; NAC, Otter Papers, Otter to Molly, 15 September, 1900.

[109] Wilfred Campbell, "Return of the Troops," printed in the Ottawa *Journal*, 7 November, 1900.

[110] NAC, Clark Papers, Diary, 31 October, 1900; Otter Papers, Otter to Molly, 11 November, 1900; Diary, 31 October, 1900.

[111] A.S. McCormick, "With the R.C.R. in South Africa," *University Magazine*, April 1901, 319.

[112] *New Brunswick South African Contingent Fund Report and Accounts, 1899-1901*, (Saint John, 1901), 56 ff.

[113] Montreal *Star*, 18 December, 1899.

[114] Montreal *Star*, 17 January, 1900.

[115] E.W.B. Morrison, *With the Guns in South Africa*, (Hamilton,1901), 63.

[116] Sessional Paper 35a (1901), 89.

[117] Hugh Robertson, "The Royal Canadian Dragoons in South Africa," (unpublished MA thesis, University of Ottawa, 1982), 189.

[118] *Ibid.*, 267.

[119] *Ibid.*, 269.

[120] NAC, A.E. Hilder Papers, "Comrades All," 95.

[121] Morrison, *With the Guns*, 270; NAC, A.E. Hilder Papers, "Comrades All," 93; RG9, II, A3, Vol. XXXII, Left Section Diary, 7 November, 1900.

[122] Morrison, *With The Guns*, 271.

[123] Canada, Sessional Paper, 35a (1901), Report C, 96; Public Record Office, War Office 105/10, Hutton to C in C. 5 November, 1900.

[124] Morrison, *With The Guns*, 258 and 290.

[125] Andrew Miller, "Organization and Work of the Strathcona's Horse," ms (1912), 15; *Monetary Times*, 23 February, 1900.

[126] NAC, R.P. Rooke Papers, "A Record from Memory," 26 April, 1908.

[127] Glenbow Museum, Steele Papers, Strathcona's Horse, Diary, 27 November, 1900.

128 Montreal *Gazette*, 9 March, 1900.

129 Neil Speed, "Born To Fight," unpublished ms, 94-95.

130 *Speed*, 95.

131 Jack Randall, *I'm Alone*, (Indianapolis, 1930), 68.

132 See Neil Speed's "Born To Fight" for a close analysis of Charlie Ross's life.

133 Canada, Sessional Paper 35a (1903) Extract from Staff Diary, Appendix A, 31 March, 1902, 35.

134 For more on this battle see Carman Miller, "No Surrender: The Battle of Harts River," 1902, *Canadian Battle Series*, No 9, (Canadian War Museum, 1993).

135 Much of this chapter is taken from my article, "The Crucible of War: Canadian and British Troops During the Boer War," in *The Boer War Army, Nation and Empire*, Peter Dennis and Jeffrey Grey (eds.), (Canberra, 2000), 84-98.

136 NAC, R.E.W. Turner Papers, Diary, 20 July, 1900.

137 Jeanette Duncan, *The Imperialist*, (London, 1904).

138 The *Globe*, 7 April, 1902.

139 Public Record Office, War Office 108/117, Confidential Memo, General Order 1329, 10 March, 1902.

140 Jack Randall, *I'm Alone*, (Indianapolis, 1931), 50-51.

141 W.A. Griesbach, *I Remember*, (Toronto, 1946), 312.

142 Randall, *I'm Alone*, 5-53.

143 Griesbach, *I Remember*, 312.

144 Public Record Office, Colonial Office, 256/24, Captain Charles Beer to ADSCO, E Division, 30 June, 1903.

145 Public Record Office, Colonial Office, 526/3/24, Pilkington to Chief Staff Officer, SAC, 24 July, 1903.

146 Public Record Office, Colonial Office, 526/3/24, Mrs. H.S. Massiah to the King, 21 October, 1902.

147 *Mail and Empire*, 11 April, 1903.

148 See, John F. Owen, "The Military Forces of our Colonies" *The Fortnightly Review*, March, 1900; Richard Jebb, *Studies in Colonial Nationalism*, (London, 1905); Arthur Conan Doyle, *The Great Boer War*, (London, 1903), 742; Rudyard Kipling, "The Captive," in *Traffics and Discoveries*, (London, 1904); John Sterling, *The Colonials in South Africa, 1899-1902*, (Edinburgh, 1907).

149 Benedict Anderson, *Imagined Communities*. For a fuller account, see Craig Wilcox, *Australia's Boer War: The War in South Africa, 1899–1902* (Melbourne, 2002).

150 Harold Spender, *Manchester Guardian*, 14 January, 1901.

151 McGill University Rare Book Room, W.D. Lighthall Papers, Lighthall to Hofmeyer, 8 January, 1901

152 W.D. Lighthall Papers, Lighthall to Hofmeyer, 18 January, 1901.

153 W.D. Lighthall Papers, Hofmeyer to Lighthall, 17 January, 1901.

154 Brian Douglas Tennyson, *Canadian Relations with South Africa*, (Washington, 1982), 14-17.

155 W.D. "Shuyler" Lighthall, *To The Boers: A Friend's Appeal From Canada*, (Montreal, 1902), 4.

156 Sanford Evans, "Current Affairs," *Canadian Magazine*, Vol. XVI, No 2, December, 1900, 178.

157 NAC, M.G. 30, E 399, Archibald Hayes MacDonell Papers, ms, 3.

158 Quoted in Richard Allen, "Children of Prophecy: Wesley College Students in an Age of Reform," *Red River Valley Historian*, Summer, 1974, 17.

159 Labat, *Le Livre d'Or*, 128; NAC, Victor Odlum Papers, Vol. 15, *Sentinel Review*, 28 August, 1900.

160 Labat, *Le Livre d'Or*.

161 Canada, House of Commons, Debates, 13 March, 1900, 1848.

162 Norman Patterson, "The War and Canada," *Canadian Magazine*, July, 1902, 204.

163 Sara Jeanette Duncan, *The Imperialist*, (McClelland & Stewart Limited, Toronto, 1971), 229.

164 W. Sanford Evans, "Current Events," *Canadian Magazine*, April, 1900, 518.

165 See, John MacFarlane, "'*Ready, Aye, Ready?' French Canadians and the South African War 1899-1902*," (unpublished paper for the Canadian Historical Association's annual meetings, 1998).

166 O.D. Skelton, *The Day of Sir Wilfrid Laurier*, (Toronto, 1920), 188.

BIBLIOGRAPHY

BOOKS

Amery, L.S., ed. *The Times History of the War in South Africa 1899-1902.* 7 vols. London: Sampson Low, Marston & Co, 1900-09.

Brown S. M. *With The Royal Canadians. Toronto:* Publishers' Syndicate, 1900.

Evans, William Sanford. *The Canadian Contingents and Canadian Imperialism: A Story and a Study.* Toronto: Publishers' Syndicate, 1901.

Hart-McHarg, William. *From Quebec to Pretoria.* Toronto: William Briggs, 1902.

Hubly, G. Russell. *G Company, or Every-day life of the R. C. R.: being a descriptive account of typical events in the Life of the First Canadian Contingent in South Africa.* St. John, N.B: J. & A. McMillan, 1901.

Labat, Gaston P. *Le Livre D'Or of the Canadian Contingents in South Africa.* Montreal: 1901.

Marquis, T. G. *Canada's Sons on Kopje and Veldt.* Toronto: Canada's Sons Publishing Co., 1900.

Miller, Carman. *Painting The Map Red, Canada and the South African War 1899-1902.* Montreal: McGill-Queens University Press, 1993; reprint 1998, University of Natal Press, 1998.

Morrison, E.W.B. *With The Guns in South Africa.* Hamilton, Ont.: 1901.

Morton, Desmond. *The Canadian General Sir William Otter.* Toronto: Hakkert, 1974.

Morris, A. G., ed. *A Canadian Mounted Rifleman At War 1899-1902 The Reminiscences Of A. E. Hilder.* Second Series, No 31. Cape Town: Van Riebeeck Society, 2000.

Nasson, Bill. *The South African War.* London: Arnold, 1999.

Pakenham, Thomas. *The Boer War.* London: Weidenfeld & Nicolson, 1979.

Porter, A. N. *The Origins of the South African War: Joseph and the Diplomacy of Imperialism 1895-99.* Manchester: Manchester University Press, 1980.

Pretorius, Fransjohan. *The Anglo-Boer War 1899-1902.* Cape Town: Don Nelson, 1985.

Reid, Brian A.. *Our Little Army in the Field: The Canadians in South Africa.* St Catharine's: Vanwell Publishing Limited, 1996.

Smith, Iain R. *The Origins of the South African War, 1899-1902.* London: Longman, 1996.

Speed, Neil. *Born To Fight.* Victoria: 2002.

Spies, S.B.. *Methods of Barbarism?: Roberts and Kitchener and civilians in the Boer Republics, January 1900-May 1902.* Cape Town: Human & Rousseau, 1977.

Warwick, Peter. *Black People and the South African War.* Cambridge: Cambridge University Press, 1983.

Wilcox, Craig. *Australia's Boer War: The War in South Africa, 1899-1902.* Melbourne: Oxford University Press, 2002.

BOOKLETS

Miller, Carman. *No Surrender: The Battle of Harts River.* Canadian Battle Series No. 9. Toronto: Canadian War Museum, 1993.

Morton, Desmond. *The Canadians at Paardeberg (1900).*

Canadian Battle Series No. 2, Ottawa: Canadian War
Museum.

Page, Robert. *The Boer War and Canadian Imperialism.*
Historical Booklet No. 44. Ottawa: Canadian Historical
Association, 1987.

ARTICLES

Miller, Carman. "A Preliminary Analysis of the Socio-economic Composition of Canada's South African War
Contingents," *Social History/Histoire Sociale* (November,
1975): 219-237.

Miller, Carman. "Chums in Arms: Comradeship Among
Canada's South African Soldiers," *Social History/Histoire
Sociale* (November, 1985): 359-373.

Miller, Carman. "Loyalty, Patriotism and Resistance: Canada's
Response to the Anglo-Boer War, 1899-1902," *The South
African Historical Journal* 41 (November, 1999): 1-12.

Miller, Carman. "The Crucible of War: Canadian and British
Troops during the Boer War." In *Army and Empire*, edited
by Peter Dennis and Jeffrey Grey, 84-98. Canberra: Army
History Unit Canberra, 2000.

Miller, Carman. "The Unhappy Warriors: Conflict and
Nationality among Canadian Troops during the South
African War." *The Journal of Imperial and Commonwealth
History* Vol. 23, No.1 (January, 1995): 77-104.

Miller, Carman. "The Montreal Flag Riot of 1900."In *One
Flag One Queen One Tongue*, edited by John Crawford and
Ian McGibbon, 165-179. Auckland University Press, 2003.

Miller, Carman, "Research Resources on Canada and the
South African War." *Archivaria* 26 (Summer, 1988): 116-
121.

Page, Robert. "Canada and the Imperial Idea in the Boer War
Years." *Journal of Canadian Studies/Revue d'etudes canadi-
ennes* (August 1970): 39-43.

Pelletier, Jean-Guy. "la Presse Canadienne-francaise et la
Guerre des Boers." *Recherches Sociographiques* Vol IV, No 3.
(decembre, 1963)

Index